FASHION
D·E·S·I·G·N

Felicity Everett

Consultant: Howard Tangye

(fashion designer, illustrator and teacher of fashion illustration at St Martin's School of Art, London)

Edited by Janet Cook

Designed by Camilla Luff

Cover design by Nerissa Davies

Illustrated by Nicky Dupays, Howard Tangye, Chris Lyon, Lynne Riding, Lynne Robinson, Terry Beard, Susan Alcantarilla, Lisa Darnell, Kathy James and Peter Bull.

Commissioned photography by Geoff Brightling

Picture research by Constance Novis

Contents

3 About this book

4 What is fashion design?

6 Twentieth century fashions

10 Inside a fashion studio

12 Designing a garment

14 Basic design styles

16 Specializing

18 The fashion year

20 Fashion capitals

22 From the catwalk to the high street

24 A-Z of fashion design

30 What is fashion illustration?

32 Materials

34 Equipment

36 Figure drawing

40 Fashion illustration

42 Watercolour and pastel

44 Inks and markers

46 Gouache

48 Collage

50 Pastel and pencil

52 Mixed media

54 Mounting and presentation

56 Finding work as a fashion illustrator

58 Careers in fashion

60 Going further

62 Glossary

63 Index

AG 86

First published in 1987 by Usborne Publishing Ltd, 20 Garrick Street, London WC2E 9BJ, England.

Printed in Belgium   American edition 1987.

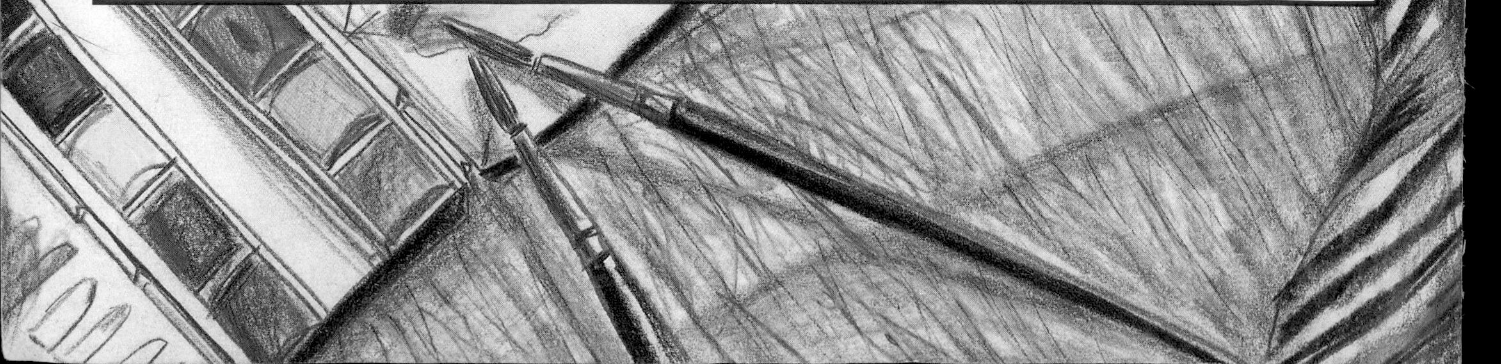

About this book

Fashion is fun, colourful and glamorous. For those involved in the fashion industry, it is also very hard work. This book takes a look at fashion design from every angle. It explores the flamboyant show-business aspect of the industry – the big names, the fashion shows and the international fashion capitals. It also takes you behind the scenes, into the organized chaos of a fashion studio, to see how clothes are designed, made and sold.

In the latter half of the book there is a practical guide to fashion illustration, covering a wide variety of artists' techniques. It provides a basis for anyone envisaging a career in fashion illustration, and is also ideal for those wanting to take it up as a hobby.

Where they first appear in a section, technical terms are printed in **_bold italics_** and explained in the glossary on page 62. The back of the book is packed with useful reference material on books, courses and careers in fashion design, illustration and other fashion-related fields.

What is fashion design?

Many people sketch clothes for fun, without considering whether they could actually be made. Professional fashion designers have to be more practical. *Their* design sketches have to work as patterns, and then as finished garments. No matter how good a design looks on paper, it is no use if it is impractical to make or wear.

What makes a good designer?

To be a good fashion designer, you do not necessarily have to be good at drawing. Some designers don't sketch at all, they just work with fabric. However, you do need imagination and a practical knowledge of how clothes are made. Having the ability to make your own clothes can be a great advantage.

Becoming a fashion designer

College prospectuses

If you want to become a professional fashion designer, the best way is to study fashion design at college. As well as teaching you about the technical and artistic side of the subject, some courses include a year working in the fashion industry, to give students a taste of commercial fashion design. Others offer the chance to visit *fashion houses* abroad. You can find out more about some of the courses available on pages 60-61.

Design competitions

Many colleges enter students for design competitions, sponsored by clothing or fabric companies. This gives the students commercial experience, and provides fresh talent for the companies. Below are two award-winning knitwear designs from the **Courtelle Design Awards.**

Men's knitwear designs for **Burton** with knitted samples attached.

Designer Alison Carter of Brighton Polytechnic with the finished sweaters.

Different types of fashion design

Haute couture

The type of design which predominated until the 1950s was **haute couture**, (French for fine tailoring). A couture garment is made for an individual customer. Look and fit take priority over the cost of materials and the time it takes to make.

CHANEL

Mass market

These days the fashion industry relies more on the **mass market**. This caters for a wide range of customers, producing **ready-to-wear** clothes in large quantities and standard sizes. Cheap materials, creatively used, produce affordable high street fashion.

benetton

Designer label

Designer label clothes are a cross between **couture** and **mass market**. They are not made for individual customers, but great care is taken in the choice and cut of the fabric. Clothes are made in small quantities to guarantee exclusivity, so they are quite costly.

LACOSTE

4

Areas of work

There are three main ways in which designers can work.

1. Working freelance

Freelance designers work for themselves. They sell their work to *fashion houses*, direct to shops or to clothing manufacturers. The garments bear the *buyer's** label.

2. Working in-house

In-house designers are employed full-time by one fashion company. Their designs are the property of that company, and cannot be sold to anyone else.

3. Setting up a company

Fashion designers sometimes set up their own companies. Many people find this more satisfying than working for someone else, as their designs are sold under their own label.

On pages 10-13 you can find out more about how fashion designers work.

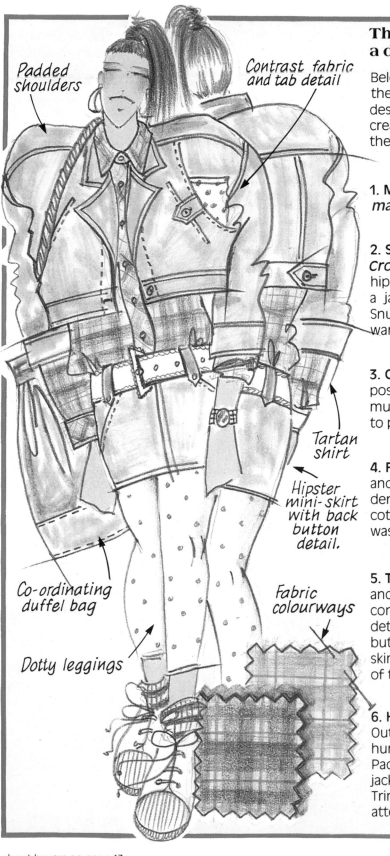

Padded shoulders

Contrast fabric and tab detail

Tartan shirt

Hipster mini-skirt with back button detail.

Co-ordinating duffel bag

Dotty leggings

Fabric colourways

The elements of a design

Below you can see all the decisions the designer made when creating the outfit on the left.

1. Market: teenage, *mass market*.

2. Season: spring. *Cropped* jacket and hipster mini-skirt give a jaunty spring feeling. Snug leggings add warmth.

3. Cost: as cheap as possible. Garments must be quick and easy to produce.

4. Fabric: inexpensive and practical. Use denim, cotton and cotton jersey (all washable).

5. Trimmings: simple and cheap. Stitching, contrast fabric and tab detail on jacket. Metal buttons on jacket and skirt. Buttons in groups of two on shirt.

6. Hanger appeal: Outfit must look good hung up in a shop. Padded shoulders of jacket give shape. Trimmings attract attention.

* You can find out more about buyers on page 13.

Twentieth century fashions

"New" fashions are hardly ever completely original. They are very often new versions of styles which have been fashionable in the past. Although fashion changes year by year, major developments are easier to detect once a particular era has passed.

It is useful for designers to study the history of fashion, as it provides a context for their work and a source of ideas. On the next four pages you can see the major developments within the world of fashion during the twentieth century.

The Edwardian era

The grandeur and extravagance of the Edwardian era (1890-1910) were reflected in the fashions of the time. For example, women's dresses were long and full-skirted and they often had *bustles*, which emphasized the hips. Styles like this used vast quantities of sumptuous fabrics such as silk, satin and *crêpe de chine*. Edwardian men wore *frock coats*, so-called because of their flared, skirt-like shape, and top hats for formal occasions.

1910

The Russian ballet peformed **Scheherezade** in Paris in 1910, in which dancers wore flowing Eastern costumes. This started a fashion for softly draped, oriental-style dresses which changed the shape of women's fashion.

The Great War

Changes in dress during World War I were dictated more by necessity than fashion. Many men wore uniform. Women wore hardwearing, practical clothes, because they took over jobs previously done by men. These conditions influenced fashion after the war.

1920s

The roles women had adopted during the war gave them the confidence to dress more boldly in the 20s.
A *couturier* called **Coco Chanel*** popularized chic, mannish styles in new fabrics, like jersey. Women wore their skirts shorter than before.

Chanel suit from 1926

Oxford bags were a popular men's fashion of the 20s. These were baggy trousers, about 16" wide at the ankles, which were first worn by students at Oxford University, England. They were revived as a women's fashion in the 30s and for women and men in the 70s.

The Bystander, 1925

* You can find out more about **Chanel** on page 24.

The bias cut

In the late 20s and early 30s, a French *couturier*, **Madeleine Vionnet** made a great technical advance in *haute couture.* She began to cut cloth on the "bias" (or diagonally, across the fabric's lengthwise threads). Her dresses therefore clung flatteringly to the body's curves.

Women's fashions in the 30s moved away from the brash, daring styles of the 20s towards a more romantic, feminine silhouette. Hemlines dropped. Backless evening gowns and soft, slim-fitting day dresses became popular. Men's clothes continued the informal, practical trend that had dominated since the end of World War I. Raincoats with military-style *epaulettes*, and *trilby hats* were popular outdoor garments of the 30s.

1940s

The Depression of the 30s was followed by the Second World War in 1939. Wartime again took its toll on fashion. Clothes became practical and hardwearing once more as women went back to work in factories and on farms, while the men were away fighting. The war brought shortages, making rationing of most goods necessary. This affected the cut and style of clothes.

The rationing of cloth meant that women's dresses and skirts became closer fitting and hemlines rose to knee-length, to save fabric. Civilian styles imitated the smart, tailored look of military uniforms. Details, such as padded shoulders, *epaulettes* and piping added variety to an otherwise austere fashion scene. When not in uniform, men wore *double-breasted* jackets, and loose-fitting trousers with *turn-ups*.

Wartime economies

Women's magazines published hints on adapting old clothes and using accessories cleverly, so that one outfit could be worn for daytime and evening. The shortage of stockings inspired some women to put fake tan on their legs and pencil in seams.

The New Look

Two years after the war ended, a designer called **Christian Dior*** launched **The New Look** (also known as the Corolle line). It consisted of a dress with a fitted bodice, flaring at the waist into a full, calf-length skirt. The style created a sensation, because its dramatic lines and extravagant use of fabric contrasted so sharply with the austerity of wartime fashions.

Christian Dior's "New Look".

* You can find out more about **Dior** on page 25.

1950s

The full skirt of **Dior's New Look** continued to be a popular shape in the 50s. Other women's fashions, such as tight-fitting trousers called "pedal pushers" and figure-hugging dresses and suits which tapered towards the knee, emphasized the female shape.

Figure-hugging styles for women.

The lounge suit was a popular item of men's formal wear. Leisure clothes included casual sports jackets and gaudy Hawaiian shirts.

Lounge suit and Hawaiian shirt

Teenage fashion

The prosperity of the 50s meant that people in their teens had a lot of money to spend on clothes. The fashion industry saw an opportunity to create a new market.

Instead of conforming to the same style of dress as their parents, young people wore clothes which reflected their own hobbies and lifestyle. The craze for rock 'n' roll music which started in the USA inspired a new teenage uniform, which rapidly spread abroad.

Boys wore blue jeans, t-shirts and leather jackets or, if they were **Teddy boys**, *drape jackets* based on the Edwardian *frock coat* (see page 6). Girls wore circular skirts, petticoats and tight sweaters, with short white ankle socks and flat pumps.

1960s

Fashion in the 60s was extreme, and the shock value of new designs came to be more important than the cut or quality of the fabric. *Haute couture*, which had dominated the fashion industry until now, was soon eclipsed by *mass market* fashion*.

Beatles-style suit

The early 60s

Men wore smart Italian suits with tapering trousers (drainpipes). This style was popularized by **The Beatles**.

The full figure which had dominated women's fashion in the 50s gave way to a fashion for skinny, boyish looks, reminiscent of the 20s. A British designer called **Mary Quant** popularized mini-skirts, coloured tights and tight sweaters known as "skinny ribs". She also developed a range of "wet-look" garments made from PVC.

Other 60s innovations included see-through blouses and dresses which had shapes cut out of the midriff and futuristic dresses made from plastic chain mail.

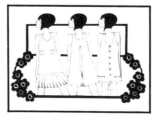

Mary Quant dresses.

The late 60s

Towards the end of the 60s, **unisex** clothes became fashionable. This meant that many clothes could be worn by both sexes. Velvet jackets, bell-bottom trousers, flowery shirts, fringed suede waistcoats and flowing scarves were all popular items.

* You can find out more about *mass market* fashion on page 4.

1970s

The unisex fashions of the late 60s continued into the early 70s. Some people took the haphazard and colourful aspects of unisex dressing and exaggerated them so that they were deliberately tasteless. This style was called **glam rock**, and was adopted by several rock bands. They wore clashing colours, glittery fabrics, lots of make-up, and shoes with enormous platform soles (see below).

Glam rock style

Another trend which became popular with women was a very feminine, countrified style of dress which consisted of long flounced skirts and high-necked blouses in traditional floral prints, worn with crocheted shawls.

In contrast to this look, 1976 brought the rebellion of **punk**. It started in England, inspired by punk-rock bands, and soon spread abroad. Punk was a threatening, unisex look worn mostly by teenagers and its aim was to shock. Punks painted angry slogans on t-shirts and leather jackets and ripped holes in them deliberately. They wore safety pins through their ears and noses, dyed their hair bright unnatural colours, wore pale face make-up and ringed their eyes with black.

Punk style

1980s

80s style has been influenced by several different countries, namely Japan, Britain and the USA.

In the early 80s, **Vivienne Westwood***, an English designer, created the **New Romantic** look. It consisted of pirate-style ruffled shirts, baggy boots and broad leather belts.

Also in the early 80s, Japanese designers such as **Yohji Yamamoto*** and **Rei Kawakubo*** introduced skilfully-cut clothes, whose loose fit and sombre colours were quite austere, yet very stylish.

Dress by Rei Kawakubo from 1984

In the USA, a craze for healthy living and sport inspired designer **Norma Kamali*** to design a range of clothes in sweatshirt fabric (which had previously only been used for sportswear). Her tops with padded shoulders and narrow baggy trousers created a triangular shape, giving the impression of a lean, muscular body. Kamali also designed the rah-rah skirt (see page 23).

In the late 80s, a renewed interest in *haute couture* led to a fashion for 50s styles such as bolero jackets, tight waists and shorter, full skirts. More tailored, skilfully-cut clothes replaced the throw-away styles of the late 70s and early 80s.

* You can find out more about all these designers on pages 26-29.

Inside a fashion studio

Most fashion designers work as part of a team in a studio (workroom). The way a studio works depends on the number of staff employed, the market* it caters for, and whether it specializes in one area of fashion such as knitwear or men's wear.

On these two pages you can find out how a design team develops a range of clothes for one season in the fashion year (this is known as a *collection*). On page 12, you can see how one dress in the collection is designed from start to finish.

The studio

On the right is the fashion studio of a leading British design team called **English Eccentrics**. They produce *designer label** fashion and knitwear in highly original fabrics for both men and women.

Here you can see the fashion designer marking out a *pattern*. Behind her are other members of the studio team. You can find out more about what their jobs involve over the page.

The design team

Claire is the company's **fashion designer**. Her job is to design the shape and style of every garment. On pages 12-13 you can see all the stages involved in designing one of them.

Judy is the studio's **knitwear designer**. She sketches shapes for her garments, then works out colour combinations and patterns on a grid. Samples are produced by machine.

Helen is the **fabric designer** She designs fabrics for Claire to use in her fashion designs. Helen sketches designs on paper, trying out various techniques like *collage* and *marbling***

* You can find out more about the different markets on page 4.
   ** The background to these two pages was marbled.

Designing a collection

In fashion, there are two main seasons a year, spring/summer and autumn/winter*. Each season requires a different fashion look and a new range of colours and fabric designs suitable for the time of year (for example, lightweight fabrics in summer, heavier fabrics in winter). To get their designs into the shops at the right time, designers have to work about 12 months in advance, so in spring, the studio will be working on the *collection* for the spring/summer of the following year. As soon as one collection is finished, they begin the next one.

Planning a collection

Every collection is very carefully researched and planned so that all the items in it complement each other, and have the particular fashion look which the company is known for. For example, **English Eccentrics** have made their international reputation designing clothes which are young, daring and witty.

Predicting trends

One of the hardest skills a fashion designer has to master is predicting future trends. To do this, they look at what the fashion directions have been in previous seasons, keep an eye on what others in the fashion business are doing, and read fashion forecasting magazines (see page 56). They also rely on knowledge of their own customers to see which styles succeeded and which were less popular in past seasons. Perhaps most importantly, designers use their imaginations to come up with new ideas. They often choose a theme to provide inspiration.

Choosing a theme

The theme of a collection can be a period in history, a foreign place, a range of colours, a type of fabric – anything which has a strong visual impact.

Vienna 1900

The theme chosen by **English Eccentrics** for their 1987 Spring/Summer *collections* was **Vienna 1900**. This theme was inspired by an art exhibition held in Paris. Visiting the exhibition gave the designers an insight into the art and culture of the Austrian city at that time and suggested many new ideas for their work.

Here you can see how the rich patterns and vibrant colours of Viennese art (and in particular the work of the artist Gustav Klimt**) inspired **English Eccentrics**' collection. The items around the edges of the book are Helen's original fabric designs and one of Claire's fashion sketches. You can see from these how the golden scrolls and geometric shapes in Klimt's paintings influenced their work. Over the page you can see how one of Helen's fabric designs which resulted from the exhibition research was made into a dress for the spring/summer collection.

* You can find out how a fashion designer's year is organized on pages 18-19.
** The book on Gustav Klimt shown above is written by Alessandra Comini and published by Thames & Hudson.

Designing a garment

Having done the groundwork, the design team decides how many and what types of garment should be included in the *collection*. The team has three months to design, produce and publicize the collection in time for their fashion show, where it will be launched before the *fashion buyers* and international press. On these two pages you can see all the stages involved in designing one of the dresses for the spring/summer 1987 collection.

1. The design

Different designers work in different ways. Some sketch their ideas on paper, others drape fabric on a dress stand, pinning, folding and tucking it until the idea for a garment emerges. Both of these two methods are shown in the photographs on the right. A third method is to adapt their own *patterns* from previous seasons (this method can give continuity to a fashion studio's output). **English Eccentrics'** fashion designer, Claire, usually uses one of the first two methods.

Two-dimensional (2-D) design sketched on paper.

Three-dimensional (3-D) design on a dress stand.

2. Making a paper pattern

Next, Claire makes a rough paper pattern, or life-size 2-D plan, of her garment. To do this, she uses a **block** (a master pattern from which many others can be adapted).

3. Making a toile

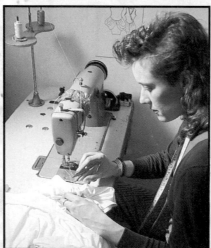

A **sample machinist** (or skilled sewing machine operator) then makes a trial version of the dress from plain-coloured cotton jersey. This is called a **toile***.

4. Trying it on

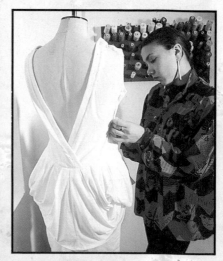

The *toile* is put on to a dress stand (or a model) to see how it fits and whether it hangs properly. Claire makes small adjustments to her original design at this stage.

* *Toiles* are nearly always made from calico, unless the finished garment is in jersey, as here.

5. Making a card pattern

6. The finished dress

When Claire is completely satisfied with the fit of the *toile*, she shows it to a professional **pattern cutter** who then makes the finished, working version of the pattern out of card. The pattern cutter's job is very precise and painstaking. The fit of the finished garment depends on her accuracy.

Finally, a sample dress is made up in the proper fabric. The finished dress will be produced in various different colour combinations (see below).

The fashion show

On the right you can see the finished dress (in one of the alternative *colourways*) as it appeared in the **English Eccentrics** fashion show in October 1986. The show was part of the **London Designer Collections** for spring/ summer 1987.

The venue for the show and the lighting, props, accessories and make-up were all carefully chosen to accentuate the **Vienna 1900** theme and to make the clothes look as attractive and appealing as possible.

Doing business

English Eccentrics invited international fashion *buyers* and journalists to the show. They consolidated the *catwalk* display by booking a stand in the Olympia exhibition hall (which is the focal point of the London collections). Here, their potential customers could find out all they wanted about garments in the collection, such as colours, delivery dates and prices. The dress in the photograph on the right proved particularly popular. Stocks had sold out by March 1987 and a new consignment of dresses had to be produced to meet the demand.

Basic design styles

Most fashion designs are based on certain recurrent shapes and styles. The wider your knowledge of how garments are constructed the more interesting your designs and drawings will be. Here you can see some of the most widely-used styles.

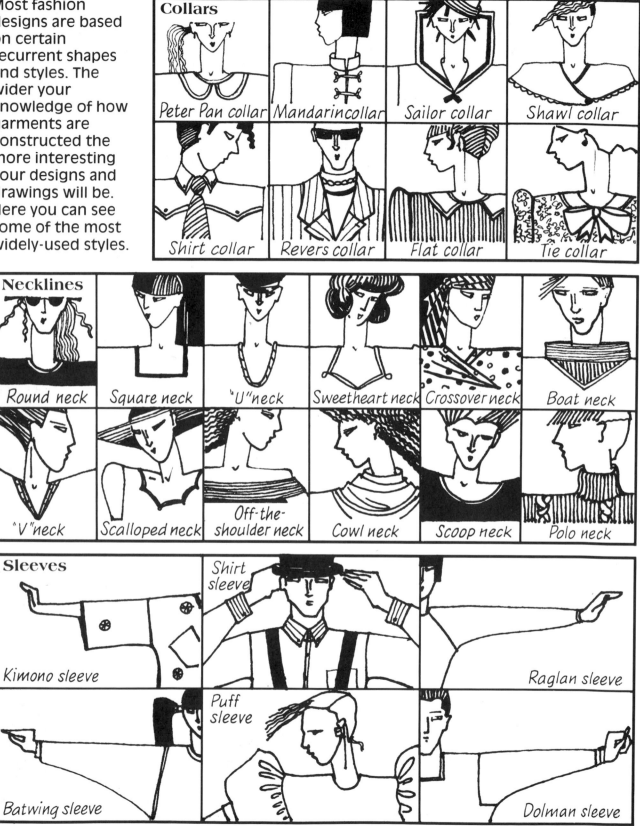

Collars

Peter Pan collar | Mandarin collar | Sailor collar | Shawl collar

Shirt collar | Revers collar | Flat collar | Tie collar

Necklines

Round neck | Square neck | "U" neck | Sweetheart neck | Crossover neck | Boat neck

"V" neck | Scalloped neck | Off-the-shoulder neck | Cowl neck | Scoop neck | Polo neck

Sleeves

Kimono sleeve | Shirt sleeve | Raglan sleeve

Batwing sleeve | Puff sleeve | Dolman sleeve

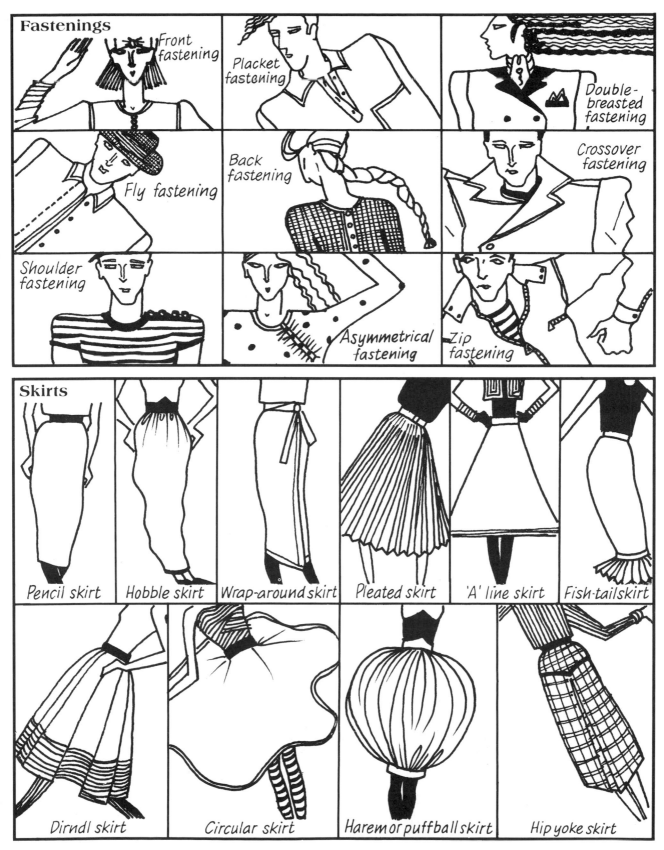

Fastenings

Front fastening

Placket fastening

Double-breasted fastening

Fly fastening

Back fastening

Crossover fastening

Shoulder fastening

Asymmetrical fastening

Zip fastening

Skirts

Pencil skirt

Hobble skirt

Wrap-around skirt

Pleated skirt

'A' line skirt

Fish-tail skirt

Dirndl skirt

Circular skirt

Harem or puffball skirt

Hip yoke skirt

Specializing

Many people in the fashion industry specialize in a particular area, such as men's wear or women's wear. The chart below shows the areas you can specialize in. Opposite, you can see why it is often a good idea to specialize.

Speciality	Sub-sections	Brief	Market	Comments
Women's wear	Day wear	Practical, comfortable, fashionable.	*Haute couture; designer label; mass market*	Women's fashions change quicker than men's and children's. Styles and colours alter considerably from season to season, especially in the mass market. *Couture* styles tend to be classic and therefore more long-lasting.
	Evening wear	Glamorous, right for the occasion.	*Haute couture;* designer label; mass market	
	Sports wear	Comfortable, well-ventilated, washable.	Mass market; some designer label	
	Lingerie (underwear)	Pretty, washable, comfortable.	Mass market; some designer label	
	Knitwear	Right weight and colour for the season.	Designer label; mass market	
Men's wear	Day wear	Casual, practical and comfortable.	*Tailoring*;* designer label; mass market	Men's fashions tend to change more gradually than women's. On the whole, men's styles and fashion colours are more conservative. Extreme styles can therefore be risky, unless you know your market very well.
	Evening wear	Smart, formal, suitable for the occasion.	Tailoring*; designer label; mass market	
	Sports wear	Comfortable, well-ventilated, washable.	Mass market; some designer label	
	Knitwear	Right weight and colours for the season.	Designer label; mass market	
Children's wear	Boys' wear	Practical, hardwearing and washable. Not too expensive (as it is quickly outgrown).		Children's clothes should be designed to appeal both to parents (who usually buy the clothes and want them to be practical) and to children who like their clothes to be colourful and fashion-conscious.
	Girls' wear			
	Teenage clothes	Highly fashion-conscious; not too expensive.	Mainly mass market; some designer label	
	Knitwear	Bright, comfortable, washable.		

* This is the traditional men's equivalent of *haute couture*.

Specializing at college

Men's wear by
Belinda Coleman

Women's evening wear
by **Kumars**

Women's day wear by
Nicollette Marshallsay

Above you can see garments from three *collections* by former students of the **London College of Fashion***. Most students produce a collection in their final year which is then shown to *buyers* and prospective employers at the college show.

To keep costs down, each collection consists of three to eight outfits (the number varies from college to college). To put across a consistent and memorable look within this limited range of garments, students specialize in one area.

Specializing in business

Many professional designers start off by specializing in a particular area of fashion. The smaller and more specific its market, the more likely a company is to get the right look and

feel to their clothes. It is also easier to establish a reputation in the fashion business if people know you for one type of product, rather than several.

When to expand

Once a fashion studio becomes established (that is, has regular orders from *buyers* and is known by the trade and the public), the design team may decide to expand into a new area. If the company has made a name for the clothes it already produces, this helps to sell the new line.

How to expand

It is safest for a company to expand into an area similar to the one it already knows. For example, a designer of men's sports wear might expand into women's sports wear. The design team can ask the advice of their regular buyers about the viability of their proposed new line.

Finding the money

If a company cannot afford to finance its growth it may grant a *licence* to a large clothing manufacturer to use the designer's label in return for payment of an agreed sum of money.

  The licensee then pays the design company each time the licence is renewed.

*You can find out more about the **London College of Fashion** on page 60.

The fashion year

The fashion year falls into two main seasons, spring/summer and autumn/winter*. Below you can find out how designers plan their time to cope with the seasons' demands. The calendar opposite shows the major fashion events.

Spring/Summer

MAR 1992 — Designer begins *collection*.

OCT 1992 — Collection shown to *buyers*.

FEB 1993 — Collection in shops.

Autumn/Winter

OCT 1992 — Designer begins collection.

MAR 1993 — Collection shown to buyers.

AUG 1993 — Collection in shops.

A typical season

Below you can see a fashion designer's diary for one season.

The theme** is the inspiration behind a collection.

Advertising the show in a trade fashion magazine attracts fashion *buyers*.

Fabric exhibition in Frankfurt – designer will attend to choose fabrics for next year's *collection*.

OCTOBER — Interstoff – book flight

NOVEMBER — Choose theme Start collection

DECEMBER — Book venue

JANUARY — Book stylist, hairdresser and make-up artist

FEBRUARY — Book ad. in Fashion Focus. Book models. Send out invitations.

MARCH — Show!

Invitations are sent to fashion buyers and the press.

Hall in which the fashion show will be held.

* Some designers also produce mid-season collections.
** You can find out more about themes on page 11.

Below you can find out about the main events in the fashion year, from the legendary *couture* *collections* to international fabric exhibitions and specialist fashion shows.

January

Italian and French *couture* collections for spring/summer (Paris and Rome)

Uomo Italia men's wear and accessories exhibition (Florence)

February

British, Italian and French *ready-to-wear* collections (London, Bologna, Paris)

IMBEX (International men's and boys' wear exhibition) (London)

International men's fashion week (Cologne)

March

British, Italian, American and French designer collections for autumn/winter (London, Milan, New York, Paris)

Munich fashion fair (Munich)

April

Interstoff clothing textiles trade fair (Frankfurt)

May

International designer collections (Tokyo)

London *mid-season* fashion exhibition for autumn

June

Italian children's wear collections (Florence)

Portex: Portuguese ready-to-wear fashion fair for spring/summer (Porto)

July

French and Italian *couture* collections for autumn/winter (Paris, Rome)

Uomo Italia men's wear (Florence)

August

Future Fashions Scandinavia Fair (Copenhagen)

International men's fashion week and international jeans fair (Cologne)

Finnish fashion fair (Helsinki)

September

British, French and American ready-to-wear collections for spring/summer (London, Paris, New York)

Mode enfantine: children's wear exhibition (Paris)

Harrogate fashion fair (England)

October

British, French, American and Italian designer collections for spring/summer (London, Paris, New York, Milan)

Interstoff international textiles and trade fair (Frankfurt)

IGEDO international fashion fair (Dusseldorf)

November

International designer collections (Tokyo)

December

Portex Portuguese ready-to-wear fashion fair for autumn/winter (Porto)

Fashion capitals

Many major cities have lively fashion industries, but only five countries have established truly international reputations in fashion design. These countries are France, Britain, the USA, Italy and Japan. In France, Britain and Japan, the fashion centres are in the capital cities. In the USA and Italy they are in New York and Milan respectively. On these two pages you can find out what makes fashion in each of these countries so special.

Milan

Italian fashions have a reputation for casual elegance and luxurious fabrics. Many Italian *couturiers*, such as **Valentino***, are based in Rome. However, Milan is seen as the fashion capital of Italy because many well-known designers are based there and it is the venue for the Italian *designer collections*, which take place at a big exhibition centre called the **Fiera di Milano** (the Milan Fair). Among the best-known and most exclusive names in

Italian style: casual, stylish daywear in sumptuous fabrics.

Italian fashion design are **Gianfranco Ferre*** (known for his boldly-cut, brightly-coloured clothes), **Giorgio Armani*** (whose subtle, mannish styles for both men and women are his hallmark) and **Gianni Versace*** (famous for his beautifully-cut leatherwear).

Paris

French fashion is chic and stylish. Paris is the home of famous *couture houses*, such as **Dior*** and **Chanel***, who stage exclusive fashion shows in their own *salons*. Many other famous French designers show their work at the *designer collections* which are held twice a year and command international attention. One of the best-known

French designers, and a pioneer of *ready-to-wear* is **Yves Saint Laurent***. He has consistently turned out stylish, quality garments over many years. **Thierry Mugler*** is well-known for his figure-hugging styles and **Karl Lagerfeld**, although a German designer, has a French approach. One of the innovators of French fashion is **Jean-Paul Gaultier***, who designs unusual, witty clothes which stand apart from the main thrust of French style.

Parisian style: sophistication skilful cutting and smart accessories.

* You can find out more about all these designers on pages 24-29.

London

The British fashion scene is known for unorthodox clothes, with a young market and popular appeal. Recently, London has attracted a lot of international attention with its *designer collections* which are held at a hall called **Olympia**.

Vivienne Westwood* is one of the pioneers of **street style** (the daring, youthful look which London is known for). Following in her wake and turning out fresh ideas consistently, are designers such as **John Galliano**, **Richmond Cornejo** and **English Eccentrics**. Other well-known names include **Zandra Rhodes*** (fairytale clothes in original fabrics), **Katharine Hamnett*** (slogan t-shirts and chic casuals) and **Bruce Oldfield*** (glamorous evening wear).

British style: young, fresh and innovative.

New York

American fashion design is dominated by a clean-cut, casual style, reflecting the sporty, health-conscious life-styles of many American city dwellers. The fashion industry in New York is based around Seventh Avenue.

A designer who helped to set the trend in America for sport-influenced day wear throughout the 1940s and 50s was **Claire McCardell**. Many of her styles have been revived in the 1980s. More recent influences on the American look have been **Calvin Klein*** (classic coats and separates), **Ralph Lauren*** (casually elegant clothes in natural fabrics), and **Donna Karan*** (practical, sophisticated women's wear).

The American look: casual, sporty lines.

Tokyo

The Japanese "look" is loose and apparently unstructured (though this can often be the result of complicated cutting techniques). Colours are often sombre and subtle and the fabrics used are richly textured.

Many of the famous names in Japanese fashion now work in Europe or the USA, but the Tokyo *designer collections* are still a major international fashion event. Famous names in Japanese fashion include **Kenzo*** (known for layered looks and highly original knitwear); **Issey Miyake*** (a master of draping and cutting) and **Rei Kawakubo*** who developed a completely new way of cutting (this can be compared with the innovation of **Vionnet**** in the 1930s).

Japanese style: loose, unstructured shapes.

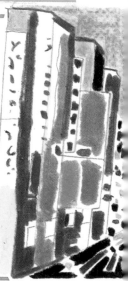

* You can find out more about all these designers on pages 24-29.
** You can find out more about **Vionnet** on page 7.

From the catwalk to the high street

On these two pages you can find out how designs find their way from the *catwalks* of the top fashion shows to the racks in the high street shops, and the subtle changes which they undergo *en route*.

Setting the trends

The innovators in fashion traditionally design for the top end of the market, as it is mainly wealthy people who can afford to follow all the latest fashions, without regard to practicality or cost. This means that the top designers can use expensive fabrics and sophisticated production techniques, such as hand-finishing and fancy decoration.

Adapting the trends

*Mass market** designers adapt the trends set by the famous names. They usually wait a season or two to make sure a style is going to catch on before producing their own versions of the original look. To save money and time, they use cheaper fabrics and simpler production techniques which can be done by machine. The end product can therefore be sold more cheaply.

Trend-watching

New *collections* are kept secret until they are offically launched at a fashion show. This prevents other designers from copying and passing designs off as their own. Once a collection is shown, it is virtually impossible to stop it from being copied. Fashion shows are full of reporters taking sketches and photographs, so a fashion "spy" with a sketchbook is inconspicuous. Designers whose work is copied have to accept the practice as a fact of life, as it is so difficult to prove that their copyright has been infringed (see opposite).

* You can find out more about the mass market on page 4.

Spot the difference

Here you can see how a mass market designer might adapt a "designer original" to cut costs and production time and to give the garment a wider appeal.

Designer original

Fully lined, double-breasted, three-quarter length jacket in wool/cashmere.

Mass market version

Jacket is same basic shape, but made from wool/synthetic fabric and unlined.

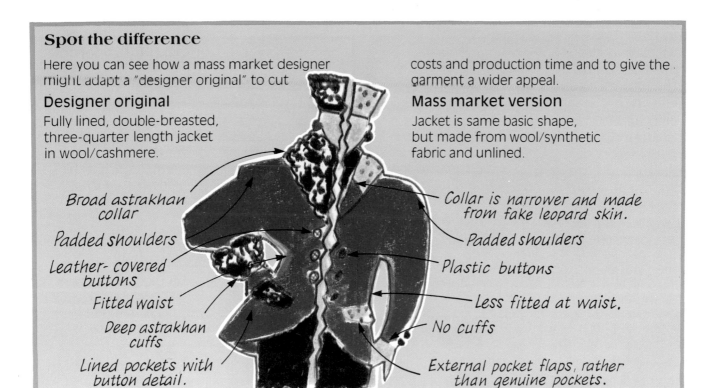

Broad astrakhan collar

Padded shoulders

Leather-covered buttons

Fitted waist

Deep astrakhan cuffs

Lined pockets with button detail.

Collar is narrower and made from fake leopard skin.

Padded shoulders

Plastic buttons

Less fitted at waist.

No cuffs

External pocket flaps, rather than genuine pockets.

Famous copies

Below are two examples of designer styles which have been copied for the *mass market.*

When Lady Diana Spencer married the Prince of Wales in 1981, her **Emanuel** dress was copied by mass market designers, who worked through the night to get cheaper replicas into the shops by the next day.

Norma Kamali's rah rah skirt was one of the most widely imitated designs of the 1980s. It was easy for high street manufacturers to copy because it was a simple design made in inexpensive sweatshirting fabric.

Copyright

In 1861 a French craft guild known as the **Chambre Syndicale de la Haute Couture** was set up to protect *couturiers* against infringement of copyright (other designers stealing their ideas). Today, even though designs can be officially registered, breaches of copyright are difficult to prove for two reasons. Firstly, the same shapes recur continually in fashion, often appearing in the work of several different designers at once, making it difficult to establish who originated them. Secondly, a designer only has to change a detail, to claim that his/her design is a different one and that no copyright laws have been infringed.

A-Z of fashion design

On the next six pages you can find out about the careers and personal hallmarks of some of the world's top fashion designers, from the late greats, such as **Chanel** and **Dior,** to rising stars like **Jean-Paul Gaultier.**

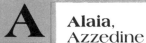

A

Alaia, Azzedine

Dates: unknown
Nationality: Tunisian

Career: studied in Tunis. Worked for **Dior, Laroche** and **Mugler,** then set up on his own.

Hallmarks: clingy, seductive women's wear in leather and viscose.

Outfit by Georgio Armani

Armani, Georgio

Dates: 1935-
Nationality: Italian

Career: designed for **Cerruti** and **Ungaro,** before launching his own label. Began with men's wear, moved into women's wear.

Hallmarks: elegant, uncluttered day wear for men and women.

B

Balenciaga, Cristobal

Dates: 1895-1972
Nationality: Spanish

Career: trained as a tailor. Opened his own salon in San Sebastian, then moved to Paris. Particularly influential in the 40s and 50s.

Hallmarks: superbly cut women's wear.

Design by Pierre Balmain

Balmain, Pierre

Dates: 1914-1982
Nationality: French

Career: no formal training. Worked for **Molyneux** and **Lelong,** before opening his own *house* in 1945.

Hallmarks: versatility. Designed elegant day, evening and sports wear.

Beene, Geoffrey

Dates: 1927-
Nationality: American

Career: studied in New York. Worked in Paris, then returned to USA to work in *ready-to-wear.* Set up his own company in 1963.

Hallmarks: witty fantasy garments, in opulent fabrics.

C

Cardin, Pierre

Dates: 1922-
Nationality: French

Career: started as tailor's assistant. Designed theatrical costumes and men's wear, then expanded into women's wear.

Hallmarks: dramatic *collections* with unifying themes.

Chanel, Coco *

Dates: 1883-1971
Nationality: French

Career: worked in a hat shop. Opened two dress shops, and later her own *fashion house* in Paris.

Hallmarks: classic women's wear in colours such as navy and beige.

House of Chanel 1987

Courrèges, André

Dates: 1923-
Nationality: French

Career: left career as civil engineer to become a designer. Worked for **Balenciaga;** started own *house* in 1961.

Hallmarks: stark, space-age designs of the 60s.

* Her real name was **Gabrielle Chanel.**

D de la Renta, Oscar

Dates: 1932-
Nationality: Dominican

Career: originally a painter. Worked for **Balenciaga**. Went to Paris, then New York, where he set up his own business.

Hallmarks: exotic and elaborate evening gowns.

House of Dior 1987

Dior, Christian

Dates: 1905-1957
Nationality: French

Career: no formal training. Worked with designers **Piguet** and **Lelong**, until he got financial backing for his own company. Presented his first collection in 1947.

Hallmarks: classic *haute couture.*

E Ellis, Perry

Dates: 1940-1987
Nationality: American

Career: studied retailing and business. Worked in sportswear from 1968; own label 1978. Own company from 1980, when he went into day wear.

Hallmarks: classics in natural fabrics.

F Fendi (company)

Dates: Founded 1918
Nationality: Italian

History: founded by **Adele Fendi** and run since by her five daughters Paola, Alda, Franca, Carla and Anna and their families.

Hallmarks: opulent fur clothing.

Ferre, Gianfranco

Dates: 1944-
Nationality: Italian

Career: qualified as an architect, but became designer of jewellery and accessories, then day wear and sports wear. Own house from 1978.

Hallmarks: chic, well-cut clothes.

Outfit by Gianfranco Ferre

Fiorucci, Elio

Dates: 1935-
Nationality: Italian

Career: ran family shoe shop from 1962. Expanded into clothes, supervising his own design team in Milan.

Hallmarks: fun clothes and accessories for the young.

G Gaultier, Jean-Paul

Dates: 1952-
Nationality: French

Career: Started sketching designs in his teens. Worked for **Cardin** and **Patou**. Own business from 1977.

Hallmarks: young, often daring, ready-to-wear designs.

Outfit by Bill Gibb

Gibb, Bill

Dates: 1943-
Nationality: Scottish

Career: trained at St Martin's School of Art, and the RCA*, London. Designed for **Baccaret**. Own firm during the 70s. Then returned to freelance work.

Hallmarks: lavish evening gowns.

Gigli, Romeo

Dates: 1950-
Nationality: Italian

Career: trained as an architect. Started work as a fashion designer in New York, returning to Milan to form his own company.

Hallmarks: soft, romantic, women's wear.

---

* Royal College of Art. For more information, see pages 60-61.

H

Halston, Roy

Dates: 1932-
Nationality: American

Career: started in *millinery*. Opened own ready-to-wear business in 1966. Has designed dance costumes.

Hallmarks: knitwear and figure-hugging clothes in jersey.

Hamnett, Katharine

Dates: 1948-
Nationality: English

Career: trained at St Martin's School of Art, London. Worked freelance. Own business from 1979.

Hallmarks: slogan t-shirts and workwear. Revived 1950s styles in late 80s.

J

Jackson, Betty

Dates: 1940-
Nationality: English

Career: Worked as illustrator. Later, designed for **Wendy Dagworthy**, **Quorum** and **Coopers**. Own company from 1981.

Hallmarks: striking, yet practical women's wear.

Women's wear by **Betty Jackson**

K

Kamali, Norma

Dates: 1945-
Nationality: American

Career: studied in New York. Opened shop selling own designs in 1967. New company, with a more sporty direction from 1978.

Hallmarks: use of jersey fabrics.

Outfit by **Norma Kamali**

Karan, Donna

Dates: 1948-
Nationality: American

Career: Trained in New York. Worked for **Addenda** and **Anne Klein** (specializing in sports wear). Set up her own company in 1984.

Hallmarks: seductive, clingy clothes such as the bodysuit.

Outfit by **Donna Karan**

Kawakubo, Rei

Dates: 1942-
Nationality: Japanese

Career: worked for textile company in Japan from 1964-1966. Then became a freelance designer. Started **Comme des Garçons** in 1969.

Hallmarks: original, sculptured designs, intricately cut.

Outfit by **Rei Kawakubo**

Kenzo*

Dates: 1940-
Nationality: Japanese

Career: studied art in Japan, then worked as a pattern designer for a magazine. Moved to Paris and worked freelance. Opened shop selling own designs in 1970.

Hallmarks: innovative knitwear.

Klein, Calvin

Dates: 1942-
Nationality: American

Career: studied in New York. Started by designing *outer wear*. Own business from 1968. Later went into sports and day wear.

Hallmarks: sophisticated clothes in natural fabrics.

*Kenzo's real name is Kenzo Takada.

Lagerfeld, Karl

Dates: 1938-
Nationality: German

Career: Worked in Paris for **Balmain** and **Patou**, then went freelance. Design director for **Chanel** from 1983. Own label from 1984.

Hallmarks: bold, often witty designs.

Lanvin, Jeanne

Dates: 1867-1946
Nationality: French

Career: trained as a dressmaker and *milliner*, and ran her own Paris hat shop. Went into dressmaking, then opened her own *house.*

Hallmarks: mother and daughter outfits.

Outfit by **Lauren**

Lauren, Ralph

Dates: 1939-
Nationality: American

Career: studied business in New York. Designed men's wear, expanded into women's wear, then started own company.

Hallmarks: casual, sophisticated clothes in natural fabrics.

M

Missoni (company)

Dates: founded 1953
Nationality: Italian

History: run by husband and wife, **Tai** and **Rosita Missoni**. They started their own knitwear label after selling freelance at first.

Hallmarks: glamorous knitwear.

Miyake, Issey

Dates: 1935-
Nationality: Japanese

Career: studied fashion in Paris. Worked for **Laroche**, **Givenchy** and **Geoffrey Beene**. Own label since 1971.

Hallmarks: rich textures, and bold geometric shapes.

Outfit by **Claude Montana**

Montana, Claude

Dates: 1949-
Nationality: French

Career: designed jewellery. Then worked for leather company in Paris. Launched own *collection* in 1977.

Hallmarks: bold, assertive clothes, often in leather.

Mori, Hanae

Dates: 1926-
Nationality: Japanese

Career: studied in Japan. Designed film costumes, and from 1955, fashions for her own shop. Moved to New York in 1977, where she opened her own *fashion house*.

Hallmarks: oriental-style evening wear.

Mugler, Thierry

Dates: 1948-
Nationality: French

Career: worked as a window dresser in Paris. First designed under the **Café de Paris** label. Started his own label in 1973.

Hallmarks: dramatic, figure-hugging women's wear.

Outfit by **Jean Muir** 1975

Muir, Jean

Dates: 1933-
Nationality: Scottish

Career: sketched clothes for **Liberty***. Moved to **Jaeger** and designed own range of clothes for them. Own company from 1966.

Hallmarks: soft, classic clothes in jersey and suede.

---

* A London department store

O Oldfield, Bruce

Dates: 1950-
Nationality: English

Career: trained at Ravensbourne College of Art* and St Martin's School of Art*. Then worked as a freelance designer. First *collection* 1975.

Hallmarks: chic evening wear.

Dress from the Bruce Oldfield collection

P Patou, Jean

Dates: 1880-1936
Nationality: French

Career: worked in his uncle's fur business. In 1912 he opened a *couture house*. Went on to design sports wear and sports-influenced day wear.

Hallmarks: simple, well-cut classics.

Outfit by **Jean Patou**

Q Quant, Mary

Dates: 1934-
Nationality: English

Career: worked for a *milliner*, then opened **Bazaar**, a shop which sold her own lines.

Hallmarks: bright, original, inexpensive clothes aimed at the young.

1960s dresses by **Mary Quant**

R Rhodes, Zandra

Dates: 1940-
Nationality: English

Career: studied at Royal College of Art*, London. Printed own textiles, which she made into dresses and sold. Own *house* from 1968.

Hallmarks: exotic fantasy dresses.

Dress from the **Zandra Rhodes** collection

S Saint Laurent, Yves

Dates: 1936-
Nationality: French

Career: studied in Paris. Worked as head designer for **Dior**. Own *house* from 1962. Pioneered *ready-to-wear*.

Hallmarks: casually stylish city clothes.

Outfit by **Saint Laurent**

Schiaparelli, Elsa

Dates: 1890-1973
Nationality: Italian

Career: studied philosophy. Designed and sold knitwear before first opening a shop, and then later her own *fashion house*.

Hallmarks: witty, imaginative designs.

T Tarlazzi, Angelo

Dates: 1945-
Nationality: Italian

Career: worked for **Carosa** in Italy, then for **Patou** in Paris, eventually becoming the company's artistic director. Own *house* from 1978.

Hallmarks: soft, fluid, women's wear.

* You can find out more about all these colleges on pages 60-61.

U

Ungaro, Emanuel

Dates: 1933-
Nationality: Italian

Career: learned tailoring with the family business. Worked for **Balenciaga** and **Courreges**. Own business from 1965.

Hallmarks: bold, sumptuous fabrics.

V

Valentino*

Dates: 1933-
Nationality: Italian

Career: studied in Milan and Paris. Worked in Paris with **Desses** and **Laroche**, before returning to Italy in 1959 to start his own *fashion house*.

Hallmarks: glamorous *couture* garments.

Outfit by Gianni Versace

Versace, Gianni

Dates: 1946-
Nationality: Italian

Career: worked with his mother (who was a dressmaker), then for **Genny** and **Complice**. Own *fashion house* from 1978.

Hallmarks: elegant, well-cut clothes, often made from leather.

W

Westwood, Vivienne

Dates: 1941-
Nationality: English

Career: trained as teacher. Opened shop, "World's End", selling punk clothes in 70s. Several influential *collections* since.

Hallmarks: shocking theme collections.

Two designs from the House of Worth

Worth, House of

Dates: 1858-1954
Nationality: French

History: started by **Charles Frederick Worth**, the first *couturier*, and run by his sons when he died. Taken over by the **House of Paquin** in 1954.

Hallmarks: gowns for society ladies.

Y

Yamamoto, Yohji

Dates: 1943-
Nationality: Japanese

Career: studied fashion in Tokyo. Worked freelance, then started his own company in 1972.

Hallmarks: innovative, loosely cut clothes.

Outfit by Yamamoto

Yuki**

Dates: 1937-
Nationality: Japanese

Career: trained as textile designer, architect and fashion designer. Worked for **Feraud**, **Michael**, **Hartnell** and **Cardin**. Own business from 1973.

Hallmarks: flowing jersey dresses.

Z

Zoran, Ladicorbic

Dates: 1947-
Nationality: Yugoslavian

Career: qualified as architect. Moved to New York. Own *collections* since 1977.

Hallmarks: stark designs in luxurious fabrics.

---

* Real name, **Valentino Garavani**.
** Real name, **Gnyuki Torimaru**.

What is fashion illustration?

Fashion illustration (or fashion drawing) is a way of presenting clothes on figures, so that they look as attractive and glamorous as possible. Newspapers and magazines use fashion drawings to show the latest styles. Advertisers use them to sell clothes.

How do illustrations differ from designs?

This is a fashion design. It is a simple, diagrammatic sketch showing in detail, with notes, how the garment should be constructed.

This is a fashion illustration of the same garment. It shows the basic style, without the same amount of detail. It also projects a good fashion image.

The beginnings of fashion illustration

The first fashion illustrations were called fashion plates. They were published in magazines from about 1770 onwards. At this time, only wealthy women could afford to have fashionable clothes made for them. In 1840 the sewing machine was invented and this meant that clothes could be mass-produced. The interest in fashion magazines became more widespread, and the need for fashion illustration was established. These days, many magazines use photographs instead of illustrations. However, the best of them use a mixture, so there is still work around for fashion illustrators.

Working as a fashion illustrator

To be a fashion illustrator you need to be good at drawing figures. You should love fashion, have a strong colour sense and the ability to draw clothes stylishly and with attention to detail. You must also be able to work to a *brief* and meet *deadlines* (deliver work on time). You can find out more about working as a fashion illustrator on pages 56-57.

Fashion illustration as a hobby

You may like to draw and even design your own clothes as a hobby. This gives you the freedom to draw the clothes you like (you could even design your ideal wardrobe). It can also be good practice if you think you may want to become a fashion illustrator. You can discover many of the basic techniques of fashion illustration on pages 36-41.

Famous fashion illustrators

Some of the greatest fashion illustrators were at work in the 1920s and 30s, before photography became the dominant medium in fashion. Look out for names such as **Erté**, **Georges Barbier**, **Helen Dryden** and **André Marty**. You can see their work in books on fashion illustration (see page 60) and in old magazines, such as **La Gazette du Bon Ton***, **Vogue** and **Harper's Bazaar**.

Later artists to look out for include **Carl Erickson**, **René Bouché** and **Antonio**.

Drawing by **Erté** for **Harper's Bazaar**

Drawing by **Barbier** for **La Gazette du Bon Ton**

* La Gazette du Bon Ton was a French fashion magazine founded in 1912.

Inspiration

Many different factors contribute to the style and mood of a fashion illustration. Obviously, the clothes you choose to draw will dominate your illustration, but other things such as the pose of the figure, the colours and textures you use, and whether you have a plain or decorative background, will also affect the "mood" of your drawing. On this page are some hints on gathering inspiration for the different aspects of your drawing.

Fashion and clothes

Look in shops and costume museums and notice the changing shape of clothes. Try to find out about fashion in the past as well as now.

Art and crafts

Paintings, sculptures and pottery can provide ideas for fabric design and decoration in your drawings. Sketch any patterns which appeal to you.

Film and video

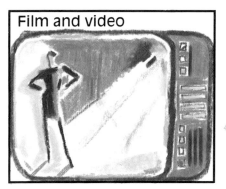

Notice the backgrounds, colours and lighting effects used in films and videos. This can help you create a "mood" for your drawing.

Books and magazines

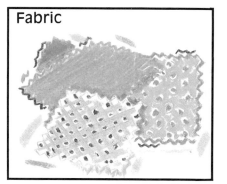

Fashion magazines (especially Italian or French ones), and books on costume and fashion will give you ideas for shapes and styles of clothes.

Fabric

Notice the textures, colours and patterns of fabric and think about the type of clothes they would be suitable for. Save scraps of fabric which appeal to you.

Making a scrap book

You could keep a scrap book of all the bits and pieces you want to save, such as clippings from magazines, bits of fabric, sketches etc.

Buy about ten sheets of strong A2 paper (it can be white or coloured). Put all the sheets together and fold them in half widthwise.

Punch* holes close to the folded edge, as shown and thread cord or ribbon through them. Now stick pictures and fabrics inside.

* If you are using thick paper, you may need to punch the holes in two batches.

Materials

On these two pages you can find out about the various materials you can use for fashion illustration. Most of them are easy to use and inexpensive. You can see examples of the effects you can achieve with these materials on pages 42-53.

Watercolour paint comes in tubes or small blocks, called pans. You mix it with water before using it. It has a fluid, translucent look which is good for loose, flowing styles of illustration (see page 42).

Gouache paint comes in tubes and jars*. It can be used as it is, or mixed with water. .Gouache gives a flat, bold effect which is good for *graphic* styles of fashion illustration (such as that on page 47).

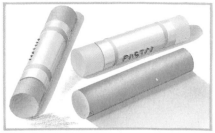

Artist's pastels are chalky sticks of colour. They come in three grades of softness and are quite expensive to buy. They can be worked (smudged and blended) on the paper to produce soft, hazy effects.

Oil pastels are sticks of colour, like artist's pastels, but they make much thicker, bolder marks. Oil pastel can be used as it is, or it can be spread and softened with petrol once it is on the paper (see page 51).

Wax crayons are harder and more translucent than oil pastels. It is worth paying a bit more for good ones, as they cover the paper more thickly. You can see a good way to use them on page 43.

Fibre-tip pens or **markers** come in many sizes, from very fine (good for outlines and detail) to very broad (for large areas of colour). Choose a good variety of colours and thicknesses to start with.

Drawing inks come in a wide range of colours. They can be put on with a brush, and used like watercolour (as on page 45), or with a fountain or dip pen for a tighter, more controlled style of drawing.

Coloured pencils combine well with watercolour or pastel. Thick, grainy ones are best for fashion drawing. Water-soluble pencils can be blended, once on the page, by putting a wash over the top.

Water-soluble crayons are chunky sticks of colour which you can blend, by adding water, to give a paint-like effect. Alternatively, use them on their own like ordinary crayons, for a thick, bold line.

* In jars, it may be called "poster paint".

Pencils

Pencils are graded for hardness or softness with letters and numbers. Below are some examples.

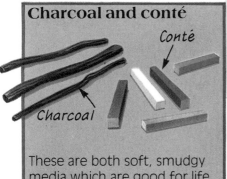

SOFT B 4B 6B 8B

MED HB HARD H 2H 4H

Soft pencils are best for most types of fashion drawing. They make thick, grainy marks which rub out easily. Hard pencils give a faint, neat line which is good for very tight styles of illustration (such as that on page 47).

Chinagraph pencils have a waxy texture which gives a thick, bold line on paper.

Charcoal and conté

Conté

Charcoal

These are both soft, smudgy media which are good for life drawings and figurative styles of fashion drawing. Charcoal comes in brittle sticks, conté in stick or pencil form. Always use a fixative to stop your finished drawing smudging.

Paper

There are many different types and weights of paper available. You can buy it in pads or single sheets, in various standard sizes (see page 35). Below you can see some of the most useful types of paper for fashion illustration.

Cartridge paper is cheap, smooth, white or cream paper. Use lightweight, unstretched cartridge for pencil, pen and wax crayon. Use heavier, stretched* cartridge paper for watercolour, gouache and ink.

Watercolour paper is quite costly. It comes in three textures, H.P. (smooth), NOT (slightly rougher) and Rough. If using a lightweight paper, stretch* it first. Heavier ones can be used unstretched.

Layout paper is cheap, lightweight paper which is good for rough work such as sketching.

Marker paper is lightweight, with a bleed-proof surface to stop fibre tip pens or markers from running. Do not use marker paper if you are also using a wetter medium, such as ink, as the paper will *cockle.*

Coloured paper is good for making collages. You can buy various kinds. Cover paper comes in a wide range of colours. Tissue paper and pictures cut from old magazines are also useful for collage. There are some more ideas on page 48.

You can buy special **Pastel paper** with a rough surface which takes grainy textures well. It is useful for artist's pastel, conté and charcoal.

Sugar paper is cheap, rough paper which comes in lots of bold colours. You can use it for charcoal, conté, pastel and chalk.

Self-adhesive film

Self-adhesive film, such as **Letratone**, comes in many different patterns and is good for giving an impression of garment texture. You can find out how to use it on page 45. On the right are some examples of textures you can simulate using Letratone.

Mohair

Rubber

Tweed

Jersey

Equipment

On these two pages you can see the equipment you need for fashion illustration. Most of it is inexpensive, except for the light box (see opposite).

Paint brushes

Brushes come in different sizes, shapes and textures. The best ones are made from animal hair (such as sable) or bristle, but you can also buy cheaper synthetic ones. There are three basic brush shapes. The round ones are the best for fashion illustration. Square brushes can be useful for painting backgrounds.

Shapes

Round   Filbert   Square

Brushes are graded in numbers, from the finest 0000, to the thickest, 20. Not all types of brush cover the whole range. It is best to start off with two fine, one thick and about three medium brushes.

Sizes

—Thin—   —Medium—   —Thick—

00 1 2   4 6 8 10   11 12

Other painting equipment

Rag for cleaning brushes and so on.

Old newspaper to protect surfaces.

Sponge for textured paint techniques.

Palette or saucer for mixing paint.

Jar of water — to thin paints and rinse brushes.

Masking tape for paint techniques and collage.

General equipment

The items below are useful for various types of illustration, as well as mounting your work.

Spray-on glue for collage and mounting.

Putty rubber — protects the surface of the paper.

Pencil sharpener

Drawing board and bulldog clip. This provides a flat work surface.

Petrol-based spirit, for thinning oil pastel.

Scalpel

Scissors

Gummed brown paper for stretching paper.

Ruler

Fixative

Aerosol fixative

Liquid fixative in diffuser

This prevents smudging in drawings done with soft media, such as pastel or conté. It comes in aerosol or liquid form. Liquid is cheaper, but you will need a **diffuser** to apply it.

Smudgers

Strip 3 in wide

These are long, pencil-shaped tubes of rolled paper for applying soft media, such as charcoal or pastel. Buy them from art shops, or make your own, by rolling up a strip of A4 cartridge paper.

Using a light box

A light box is useful for tracing a rough sketch on to thicker paper. The light shines through the thicker paper, showing the sketch beneath. They can be costly, so you may decide to make a cheaper version.

Home-made light box

You will need a cheap plastic or wooden picture frame at least 12" x 16"; a piece of toughened ¼" safety glass* cut to fit the frame (ask the glass merchant to do this for you); some thick books and an angle-poise lamp.

1

Rest either end of the framed glass on an even pile of books, distributing the weight of the glass evenly at each end.

2

Carefully position the angle-poise lamp so that the light bulb is shining up from underneath on to the glass, as shown.

Stretching paper

If you want to use watercolour or inks on lightweight paper**, stretch it first to stop it from *cockling* when the paint dries.

1

You will need a large piece of hardboard, a roll of gummed brown paper, a sponge, a clean cloth, a ruler, a scalpel, a bowl of water and a sheet of paper.

Put your paper in the centre of the hardboard. Wet it evenly all over with the dampened sponge.

2

3

Smooth the paper flat with the cloth, working from the centre outwards. Stick the edges down with gummed paper.

When the paper is completely dry, cut it off the hardboard with a scalpel, using a ruler to keep the edges straight.

Paper sizes

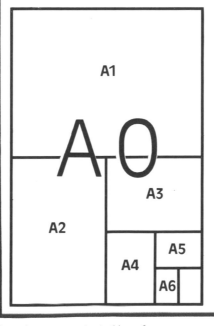

The most commonly used system of sizing paper is based on a sheet of paper with an area of one square metre (known as the A0 size). This is divided into 5 smaller sizes (see diagram) ranging from A1 which is half the A0 size to A6 which is ¹⁄₆₄ of the A0 size.

Generally, A2 is the best size to use for practising life drawing and for "loose" styles of fashion drawing. For your portfolio, and for commercial work, A3 may be more practical (it is also cheaper to buy or make an A3 size light box – see left).

* This type of glass is safe to use as long as the edges are protected by a frame.
** This includes layout paper or lightweight cartridge or watercolour paper.

Figure drawing

Clothes are usually displayed on models because this shows them off to their best advantage. If you want to do fashion illustration, it is therefore vital to learn how to draw well-proportioned figures.

The next four pages show you the techniques, from the basic construction of the figure, to a more detailed finished drawing.

Drawing from life

Your model should hold the pose for about 20 minutes.

A good way to learn figure drawing is to go to a *life drawing* class, where you will be able to draw from a nude model. This teaches you about the structure of the body. Alternatively, ask a friend to pose for you, in close fitting clothes. Then sketch him or her as shown on the next page.

Practising without a model

If you want to practise figure drawing and you cannot find anyone to model for you, here are some alternatives. You should not use them as a substitute for *life drawing*, but they are helpful because you can spend as long as you like getting the proportions and details exactly right. They will also help to improve your technique when you do have the chance to draw from life.

Magazines

You can draw figures from photographs in magazines. Resist the temptation to trace them, as your finished drawing will look flat. Prop the magazine in front of you and imagine that you are looking at a real person. Choose clear, well-lit photos showing full-length figures in interesting poses.

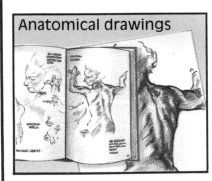

Anatomical drawings

Try copying the anatomical drawings of **Leonardo** and **Michelangelo***. This will help you learn the positions of bones, joints and muscles.

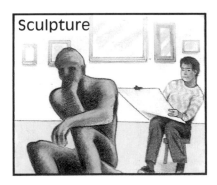

Sculpture

Draw from classical nude sculptures in your local art gallery. You can study them from all angles and spend time getting the details exactly right.

Self-portraits

Look at your face in a mirror and draw it. Or draw your own hands and feet. This will help you when you come to add details to your life drawing.

* Ask in your local library for art books containing this type of drawing.

Doing a figure drawing

When drawing from life, keep glancing at your model. The guidelines below will help you to put down what you see. Do not worry about getting the proportions exactly right. Instead, try to draw quickly and confidently. Your technical skill will improve gradually with practice.

Materials

You will need a soft pencil (6B, 7B, or 8B), an oil or artist's pastel (any colour), some sheets of A2 cartridge paper, a putty rubber, a drawing board and a bulldog clip.

Preparation

Sit far enough away from your model to enable you to see the whole figure easily. Clip the paper to your drawing board and prop it in front of you, at arm's length. Break off about 1 inch of pastel.

Method

1. Look at the angle of your model's head. Use the edge of your pastel to shade it in on your paper. This is called **blocking in.**

2. Look at the angle of the shoulders in relation to the head. Draw a pencil line to represent them. This is known as a **construction mark.**

3. Using your pastel, block in the neck (as you did the head), at right angles to the shoulders.

Right angle

Position of shoulders

CF line

Position of elbow

Right angle

Position of hand

Position of feet

4. Imagine a line running through the centre of your model, parallel to the backbone, from shoulders to waist. It may be curved, as here, depending on the model's pose. This is called the **centre front (CF)** line. Mark it in pencil. Look at the angle of the model's waist. Mark the waistline on your drawing. It should be at right angles to the CF line in the hip area.

5. Block in the upper part of the body from shoulders to waist (rib cage area) in pastel. The edges should be almost parallel to the CF line.

6. Look at your model and see what direction the imaginary CF line takes from the waist to the top of the legs. Extend the CF line on your drawing. Block in the hip area, in the same way as you did the rib cage area.

7. Before you draw the legs, look at the position of your model's feet in relation to his/her head. Make construction marks where they come. Do the same for the knees. Then block in the legs and feet.

8. Look at the position of your model's hands and elbows. Make construction marks where they come, then block in the arms and hands, as for the legs and feet.

Now you have the basic framework of your drawing. You can see how to develop it on the next page.

Adding line

Once you have put the basic shape of your model down on paper, you can use your pencil to outline the torso and limbs and position the features. This is known as *adding line.* You should still keep looking at your model as the main source of information.

Method

1. Look at your model's head. Now outline it over the top of the oblong block in your first sketch.

2. Draw a *centre front (CF)* line from the top of the head to the chin.

3. Next you find the position for the eyes. If you are looking at your model straight on, draw a *construction mark* half-way down the CF line. If you are looking at your model from above or below, the construction mark for the eyes will be further down or up, as in **b** or **c** above. Then extend the mark into a line running right across the face.

4. Notice the position of your model's nose and mouth. Make two construction marks on your CF line where they come. Now extend the marks into lines running right across the face.

5. Mark the position of the ears either side of the head, between the construction lines for the eyes and nose.

b) Head seen from above.

c) Head seen from below.

CF line

6. Working down your figure, and glancing at your model continually, outline each part of the body which you have **blocked in**. Use the blocked-in figure as a guide, improving on its shape and correcting any mistakes which you have made.

Back view Using the backbone as your guide, draw in a *centre back* line . Then use the same method as before to draw the figure.

Side view Mark in an imaginary line parallel to the model's backbone, going through the centre of the body from shoulders to waist. Then continue as before.

Proportion

Now that you know the basic technique of figure drawing, you can practise getting the proportions right. Below are some rough guidelines for drawing men, women and children. You do not have to use the "head count" shown below. Some fashion illustrators use a higher one.

Man

Eight heads high – head is bigger than a woman's, therefore figure is taller.

Woman

Eight heads high. Head is smaller than a man's. Therefore figure is shorter.

Child

The child's figure varies from four to six heads high according to age. At first the head is quite big in relation to the body, but as a child gets older the "head count" increases.

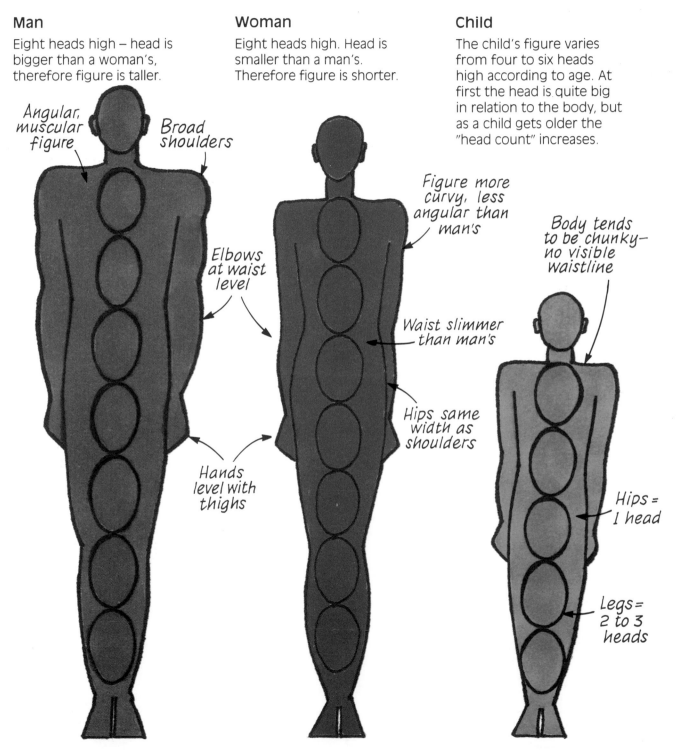

Angular, muscular figure

Broad shoulders

Elbows at waist level

Hands level with thighs

Figure more curvy, less angular than man's

Waist slimmer than man's

Hips same width as shoulders

Body tends to be chunky– no visible waistline

Hips = 1 head

Legs = 2 to 3 heads

Fashion illustration

When you have practised several figure drawings, the next stage in learning fashion illustration is to sketch a clothed figure. You may now know enough about basic anatomy and proportion to **block in** the rough shape without **construction marks**. You can then **add line**, developing your style with an eye for detail and texture as you progress.

Composition

Your figure's pose and position on the page are known as **composition**. A good way to compose* your drawing is to look at your model through a matchbox cover. Ask him/her to adopt poses suitable to the style of dress. Imagine the sides of the matchbox cover are the edges of your paper, and choose a pose which makes good use of the space. Below are some suggestions.

Women's day wear: casual standing or sitting poses.

Sports wear: active poses which convey health and vigour.

Evening wear: elegant, sophisticated lounging poses.

Men's day wear: debonair standing or sitting poses.

Drawing your figure

When you have decided on a pose for your model and the position of your drawing on the page, you can begin getting the basic shape down on paper, following the instructions below.

Materials

You will need the same materials as you used for figure drawing: a soft pencil (6B, 7B or 8B), some A2 cartridge paper, a putty rubber, drawing board and a bulldog clip. However, instead of one pastel for blocking in, you need a selection of coloured pastels (including a flesh colour** for the skin).

Blocking in

Firstly, use your flesh-coloured pastel to block in the parts of the model where flesh is visible (such as the head, hands and legs). If the limbs are covered by garments, such as tights or a long-sleeved dress, use a coloured pastel to block them in. Then block in the garments in the appropriate colours.

* If drawing from a photograph, your choice of poses will be more limited.

** Use a dark flesh-tone if drawing summer clothes or swimwear.

Adding line

When you have blocked in the shape of your figure you can define it with line, as follows:

Face and features

With your pencil, draw in the features, starting with the nose. Draw faint construction lines first if you do not feel confident positioning the features without them (see page 38). Then outline the shape of the face. Do not make your drawing too fussy (this is known as *overworking*). Use pastel or coloured pencil to add colour as you go along; that way you will be able to concentrate better and your drawing will flow.

Hair

Draw a block of solid pastel for the hair. You can add a bit of line for interest, but do not overwork it, as this will distract attention from the rest of your drawing.

Clothes

Now add line to the garments, refining the shapes you blocked in. Remember that most professional fashion drawings are done to sell clothes, so make sure you draw them accurately and attractively. Notice the "cut" of the clothes (their shape, length and fullness) and try to reproduce them as well as you can in your drawing.

Solid pastel – minimum of detail

Pattern of fabric distorted by body shape.

Add detail in pencil or coloured pencil.

Fabric

When drawing patterned fabric, such as the stripes on the top and skirt shown here, remember that the pattern will be distorted by the model's shape. Your drawing will look more three-dimensional if you draw the pattern as you see it, rather than drawing it as if it were flat.

Detail

Next, look at the details on the clothes, such as buttons, trimmings and stitching. Decide which of them add to the fashion appeal of the garment and add them to your drawing in pencil or coloured pencil.

Finishing off

Now draw in the arms, legs, hands and feet, and add any accessories such as hats, bags, gloves, or jewellery. Draw the shape of the accessory in pencil, then apply solid colour. Finally, add details in line, such as patterns on tights, buckles on bags and so on.

Developing a style

Once you have learned the basics of fashion drawing, you can experiment with different techniques until you find a style which suits you. On the next 12 pages you can find out how to use different media to produce various distinctive styles of fashion drawing.

Watercolour and pastel

This style of fashion illustration combines realistic figure drawing with casual clothes done in a soft, sketchy style, using watercolours and artist's pastels. It is a good technique to start with, as the sketchiness helps to disguise any mistakes you make.

Materials

For the life drawing: a soft lead pencil (6, 7 or 8B) or a black chinagraph pencil; a thick black artist's pastel; some A2 layout paper; a drawing board and bulldog clip and a putty rubber.

For the fashion drawing: a sheet of A2 watercolour paper (lightweight paper will need stretching* before you use it); one thick, two medium and two fine paint brushes; watercolour paints; a jam jar of water; a palette; coloured artist's pastels and a chinagraph pencil or soft lead pencil.

For optional patterns: wax crayons or masking tape.

Life drawing

Sketch on layout paper

Sketch** a friend in various poses. Work in soft pencil or chinagraph on layout paper, adding shadows in pastel, as shown above.

Now trace your best sketch on to another sheet of layout paper, adapting the clothes, if necessary, to add fashion appeal.

Tracing

Tracing on watercolour paper

Tape the drawing on to a light surface (such as a light box). Then use a 6B pencil to trace it lightly on to a sheet of watercolour paper. Simplify the lines as you trace it, and keep the drawing as clean as possible. Do not add detail and shadow at this stage.

Painting

For areas of your drawing where you want a soft-edged watercolour finish, dampen the paper with a large, clean paint brush, so that the paint flows over it evenly. For areas of hard-edged colour, paint straight on to dry paper.

Before you start painting, decide whether you will be using either of the pattern techniques shown opposite to decorate any of the garments in your picture. Do not paint any areas which you will later want to decorate using one of these methods.

1. Mix some watercolour paint with a little water in your palette. For a wider variety of shades, try mixing several colours together. Make sure you mix enough watercolour paint for all the areas you want to cover.

2. Now use your medium size paint brush to fill in any large areas of colour. Work each stroke into the last one so the paint merges and no brush strokes can be seen when you have finished.

3. Fill in medium-sized areas of the clothes, such as the skirt and hair, using the medium brushes. Then paint the small areas, such as the scarf and socks, using the finest ones.

4. Add darker tones of paint while the paper is still damp to create soft shadows (you can refer to your original life drawing to position them correctly).

* You can see how to stretch paper on page 35.
     ** You can find out more about poses and composition on page 40.

Adding pattern

Below are two effective techniques for making patterns on the clothes.

Wax crayon: draw a simple, abstract pattern in wax crayon on one or more of the garments in your picture. Then paint over it. The wax repels the paint, so the pattern shows up well when it dries.

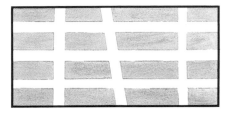

Masking tape: For hard-edged white patterns, such as stripes or checks, cut strips of masking tape and stick them down, so that they follow the contours of the body. Paint over the tape, and carefully peel it off when the paint is dry.

Adding detail

1. When the paint is dry, use coloured artist's pastels to add details, such as the woolly effect on the mini skirt, the pattern on the scarf and the face, features and hair. To get a soft, smudgy effect, apply the pastel with your finger or a cotton bud.

2. Finally, use a 6B pencil or chinagraph to add definition to your painting. You should still be able to see your original tracing lines faintly through the paint, and you can use these for reference.

Inks and markers

Here you can find out how to do a fashion illustration in a loose, impressionist style.

Materials

For sketching: a soft pencil (6, 7 or 8B) and some A2 layout paper.

For adding line and tone: a black fine-nib marker, some coloured broad-nib markers (including a flesh tone and a light grey) and some A2 cartridge paper*.

For adding texture: Letratone film (see page 33) to simulate any special textures, such as jersey or rubber.

For adding colour: one fine and one medium paint brush and some coloured drawing inks.

Preparation

Ask a friend to pose for you, in sporty or casual clothes.

Sketching

Roughly sketch your figure, as shown. If your model does not have the right clothes, choose a magazine photograph featuring appropriate garments. Ask your friend to adopt the same pose. Sketch the basic figure from life, then add clothes from the photograph.

Adding line and tone

1. Tape your sketch down on a pale surface, such as a light box**. Then tape a sheet of cartridge paper on top of it.

2. Take a black fine-nib marker and trace the outline of your sketch on to the cartridge paper. Then add the hair and face and the important features of the clothes (in this case, the main seams, hood, ribbing and boots). You can also refine the background at this stage. The pencil square in the sketch is simplified here to a single line.

3. Now fill in the face and hands using your flesh-coloured marker.

4. With your grey marker, add shadows to the figure's face and clothes.

Adding texture

Cut out pieces of **Letratone** film to fit roughly into any areas of your drawing where you want to simulate a particular texture. Peel off the backing and stick them in place.

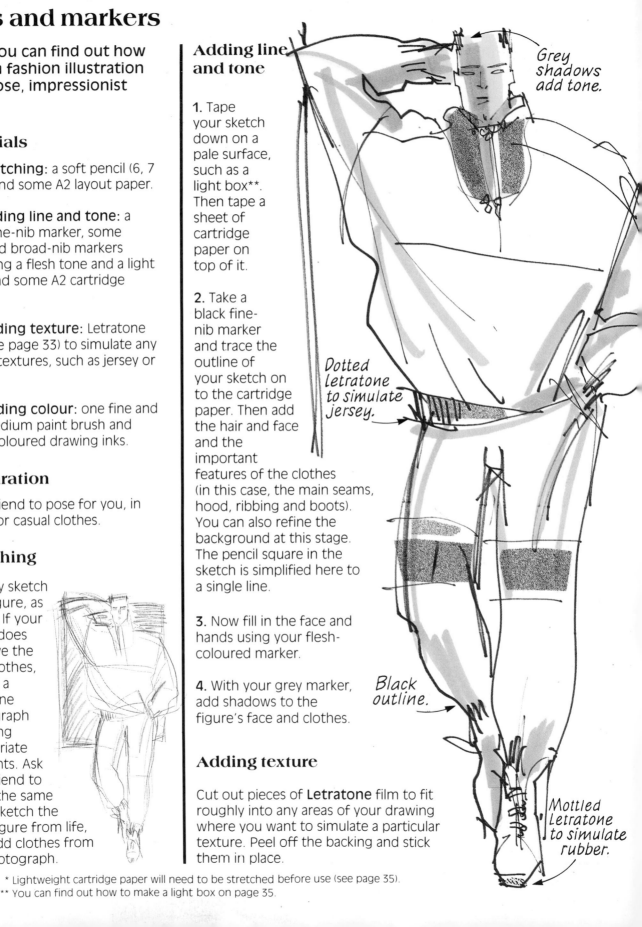

Grey shadows add tone.

Dotted letratone to simulate jersey.

Black outline.

Mottled Letratone to simulate rubber.

* Lightweight cartridge paper will need to be stretched before use (see page 35).
** You can find out how to make a light box on page 35.

Adding colour

1. Using the wider of your two paint brushes, dipped in coloured drawing ink, fill in the areas of your illustration which you want in that colour. Use bold, confident brush strokes. Let the ink dry*.

2. If you want to colour different garments, or different parts of one garment, in contrasting coloured inks, rinse out your brush in water and apply the second colour in the same way as the first. Carry on in this way until all the larger areas of your illustration are filled in.

3. With your fine paint brush, dipped in coloured drawing ink, fill in any small details of your illustration, such as the coloured flashes on the boots.

4. If you like you can add one or two flashes of colour around the edge of the figure, to give a suggestion of background and movement. Use colours which pick out the shades in the garments.

Drawing accessories

A detailed close-up of an accessory, such as a boot or belt, can add interest to your drawing and gives you the opportunity to use a wider variety of textures. Sketch your accessory in pencil first. Then trace it off in fine black marker and add shadow using grey marker. Now add texture using Letratone, as for the clothes. Finally, add flashes of colour with your fine paint brush.

Coloured drawing inks.

Coloured flashes suggest background and movement.

* This will take 15-20 minutes.

45

Gouache

Here you can find out how to do a *graphic* style of fashion illustration using gouache. The vivid effect is achieved by applying *flat colour*. You can see how to do this opposite. It is best to attempt this style when you are confident of your figure drawing skills, as your pencil outline needs to be strong, clean and boldly drawn.

Materials

Several sheets of A3 layout paper and one sheet of stretched* A3 cartridge paper, a sharp 4H pencil, a putty rubber, one fine and one fine to medium paint brush (sizes 0 and 3 would be suitable), a selection of gouache paints, a palette, a jam jar of water and a small piece of sponge (see page 34).

Preparation

Ask a friend, or two friends, to pose for you, wearing the clothes you want to draw. If you cannot find willing models, you could use a good, clear photograph to draw from instead. Plan the composition of your illustration on a piece of rough paper, including any background objects (such as the palm tree and swimming pool in the picture shown on the opposite page). You can find out more about composition on page 40.

Drawing

Using your composition plan as a rough guide and your models (or photograph) for detailed reference, carefully draw your subjects in pencil on the sheet of stretched paper.

Try to use clean, confident pencil lines, rather than rough, sketchy ones to draw the outlines. Don't press too hard – keep the pressure on the paper light, but firm. If you make any mistakes, rub them out and draw that part again.

Applying flat colour

In the finished picture opposite, there are some areas of *flat colour*. This means they have no texture or detail. Apply flat colour to your illustration following the instructions below.

1. Plan your colour scheme.

2. Squeeze some paint into your palette and mix it with water until it is the consistency of thick cream.

3. With your fine to medium paint brush, carefully fill in any large areas of your drawing which you want to be that colour.

4. Wash out your brush and add the next colour (waiting for the first colour to dry if the areas are next to each other). Continue in the same way until you have filled in all the large areas of flat colour.

5. Fill in the smaller areas, using your fine paint brush.

Adding detail

1. Using your fine paint brush, carefully paint any patterns on the clothes.

2. With the tip of the brush and a contrasting colour, add fine lines to represent any folds in the fabric.

Painting skin tone

1. Use your fine to medium brush to paint a flat flesh colour all over the skin areas. If your models have different skin colours, as here, paint each one separately.

2. When this is dry, use your fine brush to add shading in a slightly darker colour wherever you want to give the impression of shadows or hollows on your figure's skin (for example, under the arms and around the neck).

3. Now use a light flesh colour to add highlights where the light catches the model's skin (for example, on the cheek).

Adding texture

To get a textured effect, like that on the towel, use a small piece of sponge to dab a darker shade of the background colour gently over the flat colour. Apply the darker shade in lines, to give the impression of folds in the fabric.

Collage

Collage is one of the most exciting methods of creating a fashion illustration. A collage done for fun or for your *portfolio* can include as many different layers and unusual textures as you like (see below). You may be more restricted in what you can use in a collage commissioned for publication. This is due to the difficulty of reproducing certain textures when printed.

Materials

For the sketch: several sheets of A2 layout paper, a soft pencil (6, 7 or 8B) and a putty rubber.

For the collage: a sheet of heavyweight A2 cartridge paper; several sheets of coloured paper (such as cover paper) and other optional collage materials (see below); a scalpel; a large piece of hardboard for cutting on; some spray-on glue; a pair of scissors; one light coloured and one dark coloured oil pastel.

Alternative media

The collage on the right is made from coloured paper, which is a simple and versatile material. Once you have learned the technique, however, you may want to experiment with other media. Below are some suggestions.

Photocopied fabric can be used for simulating different textures. You can have photocopies made at instant print shops and libraries.

Magazine clippings, whether abstract patterns or photographs of objects, such as jewellery and handbags can provide interest in collages.

Tissue paper comes in many colours and can be crumpled, decorated with paint or pastel, or used in several layers to create different effects.

Outline

Working from a live model or a photograph, roughly sketch your figure in soft pencil on layout paper. Then trace the outline of the figure and the simplified shape of the garments on to your sheet of cartridge paper using a light box*.

Rough sketch on layout paper.

Planning the collage

Collage pieces assembled on cartridge paper.

1. Plan your colour scheme. Then put each sheet of coloured paper in turn on the hardboard and lay your sketch on top. Using the sketch as a *template* (guide), roughly cut out with a scalpel the shape of each part of your drawing, in the appropriate colours.

 * You can find out how to make a light box on page 35.

2. Now discard the cut layout paper and assemble all the collage pieces on the cartridge paper you prepared earlier.

Background

Before you stick the collage pieces down, try cutting out (or even tearing) an abstract background shape in a complementary colour, and slot it in behind the collage pieces. This can add impact to your illustration.

Sticking it down

When you are satisfied with the arrangement of the pieces, spray the back of each one in turn with glue* and stick it carefully in position. Start with the biggest pieces (such as the background shape and the main items of clothing) which form the basis of the collage. Then move on to the smaller ones, overlapping them where necessary.

Adding detail

Once you have the basic shape of the collage stuck down, you can add smaller details, still using cut paper, such as the lips and button in the illustration on the left. You do not need to use a template for these. You can simply draw the shapes on coloured paper and cut them out with scissors. If you wanted to add any accessories cut from magazine photographs, such as a pair of sun glasses or a belt, you could add them at this stage. If you do this, make sure that they are in proportion with the rest of your collage.

Adding definition

Finally, use pastel to add definition to your collage. Using a dark colour, re-draw the garment shapes, sketchily, just inside the edges of the collage pieces. Emphasize the important details (in this case the stitching on the lapels and the shape of the cuffs). Still in a dark shade, carefully draw in the features of the face, keeping them simple and bold. Then, with a light coloured pastel, add *highlights* where appropriate (in the hair, for example).

* Follow the instructions on the can carefully.

Pastel and pencil

Not all fashion illustrations feature clothes. Make-up, accessories and jewellery are common subjects too. A close-up, head-and-shoulders view of your model is best for this type of fashion drawing.

On these two pages the main subject of the drawing is the hair, and the artist has worked in shades of black and grey to give a striking effect. To emphasize the make-up, you could use the same materials, but introduce colour.

Materials

Several sheets of A3 layout paper; a soft pencil (6B, 7B or 8B); a sheet of lightweight watercolour paper, either NOT* or H.P.*, depending on your preference; some oil pastels; a small can of petroleum-based spirit for softening the pastel; some paper tissues for spreading the pastel; some water-soluble crayons; some pencil crayons and some fixative.

Preparation

If possible, ask a friend to pose for you. Otherwise, choose a good head-and-shoulders photograph to work from, which features strong make-up, interesting jewellery or an unusual hairstyle.

Rough line drawing

Make several quick line drawings of your subject, using black pastel or soft pencil on layout paper. Do not overwork the drawings. If you get the proportions wrong, start again on a fresh piece of paper. You can find out how to draw heads in proportion on page 38. Choose the rough you like best and trace it on to another sheet of layout paper. Then develop it, adding more detail until you have a good basic guide to use for your final drawing.

Now tape your line drawing on to a light box** (this is essential, as the watercolour paper is too thick to see through otherwise). Lay the watercolour paper over the top.

Shading

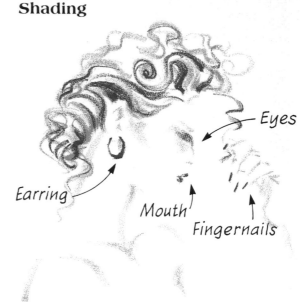

Eyes

Earring

Mouth

Fingernails

Using your line drawing as a guide, shade in the hair, face and shoulders, using the edge of a small piece of light-coloured pastel. Use a darker shade to mark the eyes and mouth, define the hair and position details such as the earrings and fingernails.

Adding line

Now take a dark-coloured pencil crayon and trace the outline of your drawing from the rough, on to the watercolour paper. Keep the line flowing as you draw. To stop your hand from smudging the pastel as you work, put a scrap of paper between it and the drawing.

* You can find out what these terms mean on page 33.
** You can see how to make a light box on page 35.

Adding tone and definition

Now use a coloured pastel crayon (or, in this case, a mid-grey) to add tone and depth to the hair, using bold, upwards and outwards strokes to give your drawing movement and vitality. Add a little dark-coloured pastel to the lips, nails and earrings to give them greater definition. Then strengthen the outline in areas such as the neck, shoulders and particularly in the hair, using a water-soluble crayon.

Adding background

Use the side of a small piece of oil pastel to shade thickly and evenly around the edge of your drawing, leaving a narrow white band (or halo) between the drawing and the background. This prevents it from looking too heavy. Dampen some tissues with petrol and wipe them gently over the pastel to soften it and spread it evenly. Finally, spray fixative on to your drawing, to prevent smudging.

51

Mixed media

Here you can find out how to use a variety of media to produce a rich, detailed style of fashion illustration which is particularly good for conveying texture and volume in fabric. The proportions and features of the figure are slightly exaggerated to add impact to the illustration.

Materials

A few sheets of layout paper; a sheet of cartridge or H.P.* watercolour paper (stretched**, if lightweight); a soft pencil (6B, 7B or 8B); a putty rubber; a drawing board and bulldog clip; some watercolour paints; a palette; a jam jar of water; a smudger; oil pastels; gouache; drawing inks; two or three fine to medium size brushes (such as sizes 3, 4 and 6); a wide, bristle brush (at least size 14) and a small can of petroleum-based spirit.

Preparation

Draw a few quick thumbnail sketches in pencil on layout paper to work out the pose and composition of your drawing. Choose the one you like best, and ask a friend to adopt the same pose for you to draw from.

Outline

Using your model for reference, begin by drawing a faint outline of the figure in soft pencil on your piece of cartridge or watercolour paper. This is just a rough guide to use as a starting point for your illustration and you should be prepared to change and refine it later, as your work progresses.

Applying the base colour

Line applied with a soft pencil.

Oil pastel applied with a bristle brush and spread with petroleum based spirit.

Using your bristle brush dipped in pastel, apply colour roughly to all the main areas of your drawing, such as the clothes, limbs, face and so on.

As you apply each colour, dip your brush in a little petroleum-based spirit and brush it over the layer of pastel you have just put down, to spread it evenly on the paper. Give your model a break while you leave it to dry.

Definition with colour and line

Now you can go on to define your figure, using pencil and whatever combination of coloured media you like (see the list of materials on the left for some suggestions). Ask your model to adopt the same pose as before, and keep glancing at him/her continually, while you add definition as shown on the next page.

* You can find out what this term means on page 33.
    ** You can find out how to stretch paper on page 35.

1. Start to work down your figure adding line with a soft pencil, and colour where you need it, as you go along. Resist the temptation to draw a pencil outline and then fill it in, as this will result in too rigid a style.

2. If using oil pastel, you can spread it on the paper as you did for the base colour. If you use watercolour, gouache or drawing inks on top of oil pastel, you will get an interesting effect, as the oil and water-based media mingle. If you want to use artist's pastels, rather than oil pastels, with paint or inks, apply the wet media first. Then let them dry and add the pastel on top.

Adding tone and texture

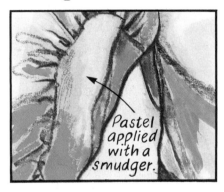

Pastel applied with a smudger.

Now go on to add tone and texture to your drawing, starting with the details of the clothes. Use a smudger or fine paint brush, dipped in oil pastel and white spirit, to draw in folds and shadows (for example, in the illustration on the right, the elbow patches and folds down the back of the shirt were done in this way). Then move on to smaller areas, such as the face, adding tone around the eyes and nose, under the chin and beneath the ear, to give an impression of shadows.

Finishing off

Finally, stand a little way away from your illustration and look at it through half-closed eyes to check any imbalance in the amount of detail in different areas. Add a bit more line to strengthen the areas which need it. Do not **_overwork_** your illustration. Once you start wondering whether to add a bit more, it is probably the best time to stop.

Mounting and presentation

Whether you do fashion illustration as a hobby or a career, your work will look more impressive if you present it well. You can find out how on these two pages.

Why mount your illustrations?

Mounting your illustrations protects them and makes them look neat and tidy.

This unmounted fashion illustration is creased around the edges and looks untidy.

Trimmed and mounted on card, the illustration looks much more professional.

Choosing a border

For a plain border, use white card or a coloured card which goes well with your illustration. If you prefer a decorative border, you could cover the card with a stylish wrapping paper, paint a pattern on it, or make a collage design. Try to ensure that the pattern does not overpower your illustration.

Positioning your illustration

Large surround   *Uneven mounting*   *Related drawings together*

The position of your illustration on its mount can also enhance its effect. It does not always have to be mounted evenly in the centre. Sometimes an unusual layout shows it off best.

How to mount your illustrations

There are two main types of mount. A **window mount** is a piece of card with a hole (window) in it, behind which the illustration is displayed. A **flat mount** is a piece of card glued to the back of your illustration. You can see how to make them below.

1. Window mounting

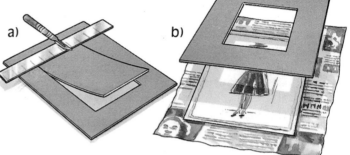

a)   b)

Try out various shapes and sizes of window, using scrap paper. Draw the one which works best on a piece of card. Then cut it out using a scalpel and steel ruler.

Cover the picture area of your illustration with a piece of scrap paper to protect it. Then spray glue* carefully around the edges. Stick the mount firmly in position.

2. Flat mounting

a)   b)

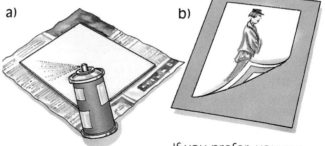

If you want a border round your drawing, use a piece of card which is bigger than it. Spray glue* evenly over the back of your illustration, then stick it on to the mount.

If you prefer, you can use double-sided tape. Stick tape along the edges of the back of your illustration. Peel off the tape backing and stick the illustration to your mount.

Protecting your work

Once you have mounted your illustrations, you could put them in a **portfolio** to keep them clean and tidy. Alternatively, you could keep them in transparent covers (see the box below).

What is a portfolio?

A portfolio is a large flat case for keeping your illustrations in. The zip-fastening ones made from plastic or leather often have ring binders, with detachable plastic wallets which are ideal for protecting your work. You can keep two illustrations, back to back, in each wallet.

You can also buy cheaper plastic or card portfolios where the illustrations are kept loose inside. If you choose this type, it is a good idea to cover your illustrations with **acetate**, or have them **laminated.** You can find out how to do this at the bottom of the page.

As well as keeping your work clean and tidy, most portfolios have handles, so you can carry them around. This is useful if you are going to a college interview, or to see prospective clients to find professional work in fashion illustration.

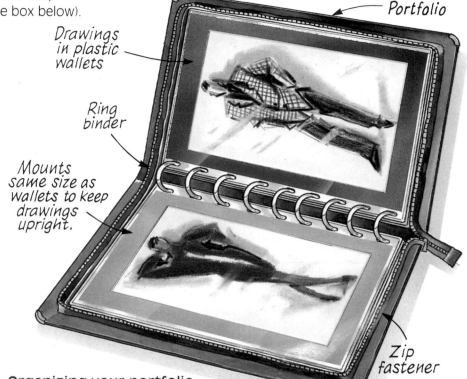

Portfolio

Drawings in plastic wallets

Ring binder

Mounts same size as wallets to keep drawings upright.

Zip fastener

Organizing your portfolio

Arrange the work in your portfolio so it looks as interesting as possible. You do not need to keep your illustrations in subject areas (men's wear, women's wear and so on).

For a college interview, it is best to show a wide range of different styles and techniques throughout. If you are looking for work, only show what you do best or what you think will be most suitable.

Transparent covers

If you want to display your illustrations on your wall or at an exhibition, or if you have the type of portfolio which does not have plastic wallets inside, it is a good idea to cover each one with a layer of transparent film to keep it clean. There are two ways you can do this.

1. Acetate

Cut the **acetate*** to the size of your mount, then tack it on with a small piece of clear tape at each corner.

2. Lamination

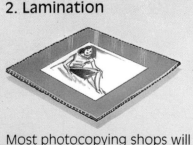

Most photocopying shops will **laminate** illustrations for you. To do this, they seal them in plastic.

Finding work as a fashion illustrator

Most fashion illustrators work *freelance*. This means that they find work with different companies. If you work freelance, your time is your own, which gives you freedom. However, organizing your work can be hard to get used to.

On these two pages you can find out about the types of freelance work available, and how to find it.

Magazines

Most fashion magazines use some fashion illustrations.* Find as much magazine work as you can at first: it is a good showcase for your work, and will help you to become established as an illustrator.

Newspapers

Newspapers often use illustrations in their fashion reports (which usually appear weekly). This is because a strong, simple illustration often reproduces better than a photograph in black and white.

Advertising

Advertising agencies handling accounts for companies who make clothes, cosmetics, accessories and so on, may use fashion illustrations in press advertisements and on hoardings. Advertising work usually pays well.

Packaging

Some companies use illustrations to decorate boxes and wrappers for their goods. Approach companies who make cosmetics, tights, or anything which is packaged in a fashion-conscious way.

Fashion forecasting

Fashion forecasting magazines predict what trends will be in future seasons, as a guide for people in the fashion industry. The fashions are seldom available to be photographed, so they use illustrations instead.

Dress patterns

Companies which produce dressmaking patterns use fashion illustrations on pattern envelopes and in catalogues. For this type of work, a simple style of illustration is required, to give the garment a wide appeal.

Chainstores

Many of the big chainstores have their own art departments, producing advertisements, catalogues and display material. They sometimes use fashion illustrators for this type of work.

* French and Italian magazines tend to use more illustrations than other countries.

Making contacts

When your *portfolio* is ready, ring up different companies in the fields mentioned on the opposite page. Make as many appointments as you can to show your work.

If you are ringing a magazine or newspaper, ask to speak to the art editor. If it is a large company, such as a chainstore or advertising agency, ask to speak to the person in charge of the art department. Find out their name from the receptionist.

When you get through to the right person, tell them your name, that you are a fashion illustrator, and that you would like to show them your portfolio. If they are too busy to see you, send them some photocopies of your work and a business card (see right). If they want to see you, note the date and time of the appointment and the person's name. Be sure to turn up on time.

If you can give a very brief description of each piece in your portfolio, saying why you did it and the effect you wanted to achieve, this will create a good impression.

Stages in a job

If you are lucky, some of the contacts you make may eventually ask you to do jobs for them. Below you can see the stages involved in completing a job.

1. Commission. This is when someone asks you to do a job. They will *brief* you (tell you what they want) and usually give you a purchase order, giving the name of the job, the fee and the *deadline* (delivery date).

2. Delivery. This is when you take the completed work back to the person who commissioned it.

They may ask you to make **corrections** to the job within a certain time. You don't usually get any extra money.

3. Acceptance/rejection. When they have seen your completed job, the person who commissioned it will usually accept it. If they are unhappy with it, they may pay you a rejection fee (usually 50% of the agreed fee for the job).

4. Payment. To receive payment you usually have to send an invoice (or bill) to the company's accounts department.

Business cards

Name, address and telephone number

You can have business cards printed, or, if you can't afford this, design your own and photocopy it. Give a card to a prospective client as a reminder, when you leave.

Managing your money*

It is a good idea to ask your bank manager for advice about managing money. He or she may offer you a bank loan to pay for things like your portfolio, printing your business cards and perhaps buying an answerphone.

Sidelines

Fashion illustration work can be hard to find, even if you follow all the tips on this page. It is a good idea to have another skill to rely on for the times when work is slack. Experienced illustrators sometimes find part-time teaching work.

If you have done a course which included either fashion design or graphic design, you could look for work in those areas too.

* See the **Usborne Introduction to Business** (details on page 60).

Careers in fashion

Jobs in fashion range from glamorous, high profile work, such as modelling, to behind-the-scenes skills, such as pattern-cutting. For some careers, professional qualifications are a must; for others, experience and enthusiasm count for more. Here, you can find out about some popular jobs in the fashion world.

Fashion designer

Description: designing clothes (see pages 10-13).

Qualifications: various degree and diploma courses available (see pages 60-61).

Personal qualities: love of fashion, imagination, an eye for colour and detail, technical skills, artistic sense.

Getting there: build up a portfolio of fashion illustrations* (see page 55) and apply for a place on a fashion design course (see pages 60-61 for addresses).

Textile designer

Description: designing fabric weaves and prints for clothes and furnishings.

Qualifications: specialist degree and diploma courses available (see pages 60-61). Also taught as part of some fashion design courses.

Personal qualities: artistic flair, colour sense, technical skill and an eye for detail.

Getting started: build up a collection of fabric designs on paper. Apply for courses in textiles and/or fashion design.

Fashion illustrator

Description: drawing and painting clothes for commercial use (see pages 56-57).

Qualifications: few courses teach fashion illustration alone. It is included in some fashion design courses.

Personal qualities: artistic flair, love of fashion, self-discipline.

Getting started: practise drawing until you have a number of good illustrations in your *portfolio*, then apply for a course or try to work on a freelance basis.

Pattern cutter

Description: drawing out and sizing paper patterns for fashion designers or clothing manufacturers (you can find out more about this on page 13).

Qualifications: formal training is absolutely essential. Diploma courses are available at a number of colleges. Pattern cutting is also taught as part of most fashion design diploma and degree courses.

Personal qualities: fashion sense, patience, dexterity and a good eye for detail.

Getting started: apply for a place on a course in either pattern cutting or fashion design.

Teacher of fashion design or illustration

Description: teaching students of fashion design, fashion illustration or both at degree or diploma level or at evening classes.

Qualifications: degree or diploma in fashion design and experience in the fashion industry.

Personal qualities: artistic flair, love of fashion and awareness of its trends, enthusiasm, patience and the ability to communicate.

Getting there: maintain contacts in fashion education while acquiring commercial experience. Start by teaching part-time.

Fashion photographer

Description: photographing clothes on fashion models for use in newspapers, magazines or advertisements.

Qualifications: degree and diploma courses available, but not essential.

Personal qualities: artistic flair, an eye for colour, detail and composition, and a lively, outgoing personality.

Getting there: apply for photography courses or a job as an assistant to an established photographer (not necessarily in fashion photography – general experience is also useful). Build up a portfolio of your best fashion shots.

* Applicants are not expected to have done any actual fashion design before going to college.

Fashion journalist

Description: writing fashion articles for newspapers and magazines.

Qualifications: some experience of journalism is useful. Degree and diploma courses are available in journalism, media and communications. A number of fashion courses also have fashion journalism options.

Personal qualities: a good writing style, an interest in fashion, tenacity, enthusiasm and the ability to research a subject extremely thoroughly.

Getting started: apply for courses in journalism or gain reporting experience by getting a job in mainstream journalism.

Public relations consultant

Description: providing publicity and information about fashion designers, manufacturers and retailers to the press and potential customers.

Qualifications: these are not essential. Some business studies courses include public relations as an option.

Personal qualities: business sense, good communication skills, tact, dynamism and initiative.

Getting there: apply for courses in public relations or business studies courses which offer public relations as part of the training. Alternatively, apply for any kind of job with a public relations company to get experience.

Fashion model

Description: modelling clothes for photographs or at fashion shows.

Qualifications: none. Some modelling courses teach grooming and deportment, but unless you have the looks and figure for it, training is a waste of time.

Personal qualities: figure, looks and age are the essential factors. Modelling is a short-lived career. The earlier you start, the better your chances. Only the most famous and successful models go on working into their thirties. As well as having good looks, models need patience, good humour, energy and the ability to communicate.

Boys must be at least 5' 10" tall, with a medium build (neither fat nor thin) and good looks. They must start their modelling careers between the ages of 16 and 22.

Girls must be between 5' 8" and 5' 10" tall and must take size 10* or 12** clothes. Good looks and clear skin are essential. Well-cut hair and good fingernails are an asset. Girls must start modelling between the ages of 16 and 20.

Getting there: send a good, clear, full-length photograph and a close-up head and shoulders shot of yourself to some reputable modelling agencies. Write your name, age, height and size on the back, and enclose a stamped, self-addressed envelope.

Fashion buyer

Description: responsible for ordering stocks of clothes for shops, especially the larger chain stores.

Qualifications: none essential. Some business schools run courses on retailing which cover buying.

Personal qualities: an interest in fashion, a strong colour sense and an eye for detail; a good business sense, initiative.

Getting there: a degree in any subject is a basic requirement of most retailers who are recruiting buying trainees. Business studies which include retailing would be especially useful.

Stylist

Description: co-ordinating the clothes, jewellery, accessories and so on, used in fashion photographs and catwalk shows.

Qualifications: none. Most stylists move into styling via other fashion careers, such as designing.

Personal qualities: love of fashion, a very good colour sense, an eye for detail, energy and diplomacy.

Getting there: build up a portfolio of fashion shots which you have styled. You may get the chance to do this by working as an assistant to an established stylist, or photographer.

* European size 38, US size 8
** European size 40, US size 10

Going further

If you would like to find out more about any aspect of fashion, the books and selected courses listed on these two pages will give you a good starting point.

Book list

Fashion: general

Couture: The Great Fashion Designers
Caroline Rennolds Milbank
Thames & Hudson
(published in the USA under the imprint
Stewart, Tabori & Chang)

Karl Lagerfeld: A Fashion Journal
Anna Piagi
Thames & Hudson
(published in the USA under the imprint
Weidenfeld & Nicholson)

Seasons
Bruce Oldfield
Pan Books

The Encyclopaedia of Fashion
Georgina O'Hara
Thames & Hudson
(published in the USA under the imprint
Abrams)

Yves Saint Laurent
Yves Saint Laurent et al
Thames & Hudson
(published in the USA under the imprint
Clarkson Potter)

Fashion design

Encyclopedia of Fashion Details
Patrick John Ireland
Batsford

Erté Fashion Designs
Erté
Dover

Fashion Design and Illustration I
John M. Turnpenny
Hutchison

Fashion Design Drawing and Presentation
Patrick John Ireland
Batsford

History of fashion

Adorned in Dreams: Fashion and
Modernity
Elizabeth Wilson
Virago
(published in the USA under the imprint
University of California Press)

A History of Fashion
J. Anderson Black & Madge Garland
Orbis

Costume and Fashion: a Concise History
James Laver
Thames & Hudson
(published in the USA under the imprint
Thames & Hudson Inc.)

History of 20th Century Fashion
Elizabeth Ewing
Batsford
(published in the USA under the imprint
Barnes & Noble)

The History of Haute Couture 1850-1950
Diana de Marly
Batsford
(published in the USA under the imprint
Holmes & Meier)

Fashion illustration

Figure Drawing for Fashion
Isao Yajima
Graphic-Sha

Fashion Drawing in Vogue
William Packer
Thames & Hudson
(published in the USA under the imprint
Putnam Publishers)

Fashion Illustration in New York
Peter Sato
Graphic-sha

Fashion in Paris
From the "Journal des Dames des Modes"
1912-1913
Thames & Hudson
(published in the USA under the imprint
Rizzoli Publishers)

From the Ballet Russes to Vogue
The Art of Georges Lepape
Claude Lepape & Thierry Defert
Thames & Hudson
(published in the USA under the imprint
Vendome)

Business and careers

Usborne Introduction to Business
Janet Cook
Usborne Publishing

Careers in Fashion (2nd Edition)
Carole Chester
Kogan Page

Fashion courses

UK Courses

Brighton Polytechnic
Mithras House, Lewes Road
Brighton BN2 4AT.

Offers: B.A. (Hons) in Fashion Textiles with
Administration

Chelsea School of Art
Manresa Road, Chelsea
London SW3 6LS.

Offers: Foundation Course* in Art and
Design; B/TEC National Diploma in General
Art and Design; B/TEC Higher National
Diploma in Textile Design

**Eastbourne College of Arts and
Technology**
St Anne's Road, Eastbourne
East Sussex BN21 2HS.

Offers: B/TEC National Diploma in General
Vocational Design;
Dip.CSD (Chartered Society of Designers)
courses in Printed Textiles,
Constructed Textiles and Fashion Design

Epsom School of Art and Design
Ashley Road, Epsom
Surrey KT18 5BE.

Offers: B/TEC National Diploma in
Fashion; B/TEC Higher National Diploma in
Fashion Design

Harrow College of Higher Education
Northwick Park,
Harrow HA1 3TP.

Offers: B.A. (Hons) in Fashion

Kingston Polytechnic
Knights Park
Kingston-upon-Thames
Surrey KT1 2QJ.

Offers: Foundation course* in Art and
Design; B.A. (Hons) Fashion

London College of Fashion
20 John Prince's Street,
Oxford Street, London W1M 0BJ.

Offers: B/TEC National Diploma in
Fashion; B/TEC National Diploma in
Fashion/Embroidery; B/TEC Higher
National Diploma in Fashion; B/TEC
National Diploma – The Business of Fashion

Medway College of Design
Fort Pitt, Rochester
Kent ME1 1DZ.

Offers: B/TEC National Diploma in Design;
B/TEC Higher National Diploma in
Design

Middlesex Polytechnic
Cat Hill, Barnet,
Hertfordshire EN4 8HT.

Offers: B.A. (Hons) in Printed Textiles;
Constructed Textiles; Fashion Design

North East London Polytechnic
Romford Road, Stratford
London E15 4LZ.

Offers: 4 year B.A. (Hons) sandwich
course in Fashion Design with
Marketing

**Ravensbourne College of Design and
Communication**
Walden Road, Chislehurst
Bromley
Kent BR7 5NS.

Offers: Foundation Course* in Fashion;
B.A. Hons in Fashion Design

* Foundation courses are broadly-based and usually last for one year. They prepare school-leavers for higher
education at degree or diploma level.

Royal College Of Art
Kensington Gore
London SW7 2EU.
Offers: MDes (RCA) in Fashion Design; MA (RCA) in Textile Design

Faculty of Art and Design
Southampton Institute of Higher Education
East Park Terrace
Southampton SO9 4WW.
Offers: B/TEC National Diploma in Fashion Design; B/TEC Higher National Diploma in Fashion Design; B/TEC National Certificate in Fashion

St Martin's School of Art
107 Charing Cross Road,
London WC2H 0DH.
Offers: 3 year full-time B.A. (Hons) in Fashion; 4 year sandwich B.A. (Hons) in Fashion; 2 year full-time M.A. in Fashion

Trent Polytechnic Nottingham
Penn House, 9 Broad Street
Hereford HR4 9AP.
Offers: B.A. (Hons) in Fashion; B.A. (Hons) in Textiles; B.A. (Hons) in Knitwear and Fabric Design

Winchester School of Art
Park Avenue, Winchester
Hampshire SO23 8DL.
Offers: B.A. (Hons) in Textiles/Fashion; B.A. (Hons) in Textiles/Fashion (50/50 option); B.A. (Hons) in Textiles/Fashion with extended design history studies

US Courses

Art Institute of Atlanta
3376 Peachtree Road, N.E.
Atlanta, Georgia 30326, USA.
Offers: Majors in Fashion Illustration and Fashion Merchandising

Bauder Fashion College
300 Biscayne Blvd Way
Miami, Florida 33131, USA.
Offers: Associate Degree in Fashion Design

Bauder Fashion College
3355 Lennox Road, N.E.
Atlanta, Georgia 30326, USA.
Offers: Associate Degree in Fashion Design

Cornell University
Ithaca, New York 14853
USA.
Offers: Bachelor in Textile Design

Ellsworth Community College
1100 College Ave.
Iowa Falls, Iowa 50126
USA.
Offers: Associate Degree in Fashion Design

Fashion Institute of Design and Marketing

a) 818 West 7th St
Los Angeles, California 90017
USA

b) 790 Market St
San Francisco, California 94102
USA
Both offer: Certificate and Degree courses in Fashion Design and Textile Design

Fashion Institute of Technology
227 W.27th Street
New York, NY 10001, USA.
Offers: Associate Degree in Fashion Design; Bachelor in Textile Design; Bachelor of Fine Arts (specializing in Fashion Design or Fashion and Related Industries)

French Fashion Academy
600 Madison Ave.
New York, NY 10022
USA.
Offers: Certificate in Fashion Design

Louise Salinger Academy of Fashion
101 Jessie St
San Francisco, California 94105
USA.
Offers: Associate Degree in Fashion Design

Mayer School of Fashion
64 W.36th Street
New York, NY 10018, USA.
Offers: Certificate in Fashion Design

Parsons School of Design
560 7th Avenue
New York, NY 10018
USA
Offers: Bachelor of Fine Arts in Fashion Illustration.

Philadelphia College of Textiles and Science
Philadelphia, Pennsylvania 19144
USA.
Offers: Bachelors in Textile Design

Tracey-Warner School of Fashion Design
401 N. Broad St
Philadelphia, Pennsylvania 19108
USA.
Offers: Associate Degree in Fashion Design

University of California
Davis, California 95616, USA.
Offers: Bachelor in Textile Design

Virginia Marti School of Fashion Design
11308 Detroit Ave.
Cleveland, Ohio 44102, USA.
Offers: Diploma in Fashion Design

Canadian Courses

Capilano College
2055 Purcell Way
North Vancouver
British Columbia
V7J 3H5 Canada
Offers: course in Fashion

College Lasalle
2015 rue Drummond
Montreal, Quebec
H3G 1W7 Canada.
Offers: course in Fashion Design

Fanshawe College of Applied Arts and Technology
1460 Oxford Street East
London, Ontario
N5W 5H1 Canada.
Offers: course in Fashion Design

Fraser Valley College
45600 Airport Road
Chilliwack, British Columbia
V2P 6R4 Canada.
Offers: course in Fashion Design

George Brown College of Applied Arts and Technology
Box 1015 Station B
Toronto, Ontario
M5T 2T9 Canada.
Offers: course in Creative Fashion Design

Ryerson Polytechnical Institute
350 Victoria Street
Toronto, Ontario
M5B 2K3 Canada.
Offers: Diploma in Fashion

Sheridan College of Applied Arts and Technology
Trafalgar Road
Oakville, Ontario, L6H 2L1 Canada.
Offers: course in Fashion Technique and Design

New Zealand courses

Wellington Polytechnic
Private Bag
Wellington, New Zealand.
Offers: Certificate in Clothing and Textiles; Diploma in Textile Design

Australian courses

Curtin University of Technology
Perth, Western Australia.
Offers: B.A. in Design

Riverina-Murray Institute of Higher Education
Wagga Campus
Boorooma Street, North Wagga Wagga
NSW 2650, Australia.
Offers: Bachelor of Visual Arts degree in Textiles

Queensland House
Seven Hills College
Division of Technical and Further Education
59 Peel Street
South Brisbane 4101, Australia.
Offers: B.A. in Fashion; B.A. in Textile Design

Sydney College of the Arts
P.O. Box 226
Glebe 2037, Sydney, Australia.
Offers: B.A. in Fashion and Textile Design

Glossary

Acetate: clear plastic film.

Adding line: in figure drawing, using pencil to outline torso and limbs, and position features.

Block: a master pattern from which others can be adapted.

Blocking in: in figure drawing, shading in the model's shape.

Brief: concise instructions, provided for a particular piece of work, which must be followed precisely.

Bustle: a pad worn under a long, full skirt, attached to the back below waist level, to emphasize the hips.

Buyer: see fashion buyer.

Catwalk: a raised platform used to present a fashion show.

Centre back: line running through the centre of a figure.

Centre front (CF): line running through the centre of a figure, parallel to the backbone.

Cockle: a wrinkle or pucker in a sheet of paper.

Collage: an illustration made of layers of coloured paper and other materials.

Collection: a range of co-ordinated clothes.

Colourways: the choice of alternative colours or colour combinations for a garment.

Composition: in figure drawing, the pose and position of a figure on the page.

Construction marks: in figure drawing, marks made to show the position of features and the angles of the body.

Couture: see *haute couture.*

Couturiers: the designers of *haute couture.*

Crêpe de chine: raw silk fabric with a crinkled texture.

Cropped: a short version of a garment; for example, a jacket ending at the waist.

Deadline: the latest time by which work may be delivered.

Designer label: well-made garments produced in small quantities.

Diffuser: a device for spraying liquid (such as fixative) evenly over an illustration.

Double-breasted: a garment with overlapping fronts, fastened with two rows of buttons.

Drape jacket: a long jacket of generous cut, with a single, low-buttoned fastening.

Epaulette: a decorative shoulder strap.

Fashion buyer: someone who selects and orders clothes from fashion houses for sale in shops and stores.

Fashion houses: established fashion design companies.

Flat colour: an even spread of colour, with no texture or detail.

Freelance: illustrator or designer who finds work with different companies.

Frock coat: a knee-length man's coat, with a flared skirt.

Graphic: vivid, life-like style of drawing or painting.

Haute couture (French for fine tailoring): a garment made for an individual customer.

Highlights: in drawing, light tone to emphasise prominent features.

House: see fashion house.

Laminate: to seal an illustration or photograph between two sheets of clear plastic.

Licence: an agreement whereby a large clothing manufacturer uses a designer's label for an agreed sum.

Life drawing: drawing human figures from live models.

Marbling: a mottled effect on paper, resembling marble.

Mass market: cheaply produced, ready-to-wear garments.

Mid-season: extra collection produced half-way through the spring/summer or autumn/winter collections.

Millinery: the design and making of hats.

Outer wear: garments worn outdoors, such as coats and jackets.

Overworking: in drawing, spoiling an illustration by adding too much detail.

Oxford bags: baggy trousers with wide bottoms.

Pattern: a diagram used as a guide for cutting out garments.

Pattern cutter: a skilled operator who draws out and sizes the working version of the pattern.

Portfolio: a large flat case in which illustrations are stored.

Ready-to-wear: garments produced in bulk for a wide range of customers.

Salon: a large room in *couture* houses, where exclusive fashion shows are presented.

Sample machinist: a skilled sewing machine operator who makes up the first version of a garment.

Tailoring: cutting, styling and hand-making a well-finished garment.

Template: a guide or pattern.

Toile: trial version of a garment, usually made in calico.

Trilby hat: a soft felt hat, with a dented crown and flexible brim.

Turn-up: a turned up fold at the bottom of a trouser leg.

Index

accessories, how to draw, 45
acetate covers, 55
adding line, 38, 40, 41, 50
advertising, working for, 56
Alaia, Azzedine, 24
American fashion, 21
anatomical drawings, 36
Antonio, 30
Armani, Giorgio, 20, 24
artist's pastels, 32

background, to illustrations, 45, 46, 47, 49, 51
Balenciaga, Cristobal, 24
Balmain, Pierre, 24
Barbier, Georges, 30
Beatles, The, 8
Beene, Geoffrey, 24
bias cut, 7
block (master pattern), 12
blocking in, 37, 38, 40
book list, 60
books, using ideas from, 31
border, for mounts, 54
Bouché, René, 30
boys' wear, 16
brief, design, 30, 57
British fashion, 21
brushes, 34
business cards, 57
bustles, 6
Bystander, The, 6

Cardin, Pierre, 24
careers in fashion, 58-59
cartridge paper, 33
catwalk displays, 13, 22
centre back line, 38
centre front (CF) line, 37, 38
chainstores, working for, 56
chalks, 32
Chanel, Coco, 6, 20, 24
charcoal, 33
children's wear, 16
Chinagraph pencils, 33

cockling, 33, 35
collage, 33, 48-49
collections, 10, 11, 18, 19
    designing, 11
    new, 22
    planning, 11
coloured paper, 33
coloured pencils, 32
colourways, 13
Comme des Garçons, 26
commissioned illustrations, 57
company, setting up a, 5, 17
competitions, design, 4
composition, 40, 46
construction marks/lines, 37, 38, 40, 41
contacts, 57
conté, 33
copies, of collections, 23
copying collections, 22
copyright of designs, 23
Cornejo, Richmond, 21
Courrèges, André, 24
couture see haute couture
cut, of clothes, 41

day wear, 16, 40
deadlines, 30, 57

definition, in illustrations, 49, 51, 52
de la Renta, Oscar, 25
design
    basic styles, 14-15
    elements of, 5
    of a garment, 12-13
design team 10-11
designer collections, 19, 20, 21
designer, fabric see fabric designer
designer, fashion see fashion designer
designer label, 4
detail, how to draw, 41, 43, 46
Dior, Christian, 7, 8, 20, 25
dip pen, 32
drainpipes, 8
drape jackets, 8
draping designs, 12
drawing, 46
drawing inks, 32
dress pattern companies, working for, 56
Dryden, Helen, 30

Ellis, Perry, 25
Emanuel, 23
English Eccentrics, 10, 11, 12, 13, 21
equipment, illustration, 34-35
Erickson, Carl, 30

Erté, 30
evening wear, 16, 40
expansion, of a studio, 17

fabric, 31
fabric design, ideas for, 31
fabric design/designer, 10
    see also textile designer
fabric, how to draw, 41
fashion buyers, 12, 13, 17, 18
    career information, 59
fashion courses, 60-61
fashion,
    designer, 4, 10, 30
    areas of work, 5
    career information, 58
fashion forecasting magazines, 11, 56
fashion houses, 4, 5
fashion illustration, 30-31, 40-41
    career information, 58
    finding work, 56-57
    ideas for, 31
fashion journalist, career information, 59
fashion model, career information, 59
fashion photographer, career information, 58
fashion plates, 30
fashion shows, 13, 22
fashion year, 10, 11, 18, 19
Fendi, 25
Ferre, Gianfranco, 20, 25
fibre-tip pens, 32
figure drawing, 36-39
film, self-adhesive, 33
films, using ideas from, 31
financing, 17, 57
Fiorucci, Elio, 25
fixative, 33, 34
flat colour, 46, 47
flat mounting, 54
framework, basic of life model drawing, 37
freelance
    designers, 5
    fashion illustrators, 56
French fashion, 20

Galliano, John, 21
Gaultier, Jean-Paul, 20, 25
Gazette du Bon Ton, 30
Gibb, Bill, 25
Gigli, Romeo, 25
girls' wear, 16
glam rock, 9
glue, spray-on, 34
gouache illustration, 46-47
gouache paint, 32
graphic style, 32, 46

hair, how to draw, 41, 50-51
Halston, Roy, 26
Hamnett, Katharine, 21, 26
hanger appeal, 5
Harper's Bazaar, 30
haute couture, 4, 16
    collections, 19
head count, proportion in figure drawing, 39
highlights, 49

illustration styles, 32, 42, 46, 48, 50, 52
ink, drawing, 32
ink illustrations, 44-45
Italian fashion, 20

Jackson, Betty, 26
Japanese fashion, 21
journalist, fashion see fashion journalist

Kamali, Norma, 9, 23, 26
Karan, Donna, 21, 26
Kawakubo, Rei, 9, 21, 26
Kenzo, 21, 26
Klein, Calvin, 21, 26
Klimt, Gustav, 11
knitwear, 16
knitwear designer, 10

Lagerfeld, 20, 27
laminated covers, 55
Lanvin, Jeanne, 27
Lauren, Ralph, 21, 27
layout paper, 33
Leonardo, 36
Letratone self-adhesive film, 33, 44, 45
licensing of designs, 17
life drawing class, 36
light box, 35
lightweight paper, 33, 35
lingerie, 16
London, 21

magazines
    using ideas from, 31, 36, 48
    working for, 58
marker illustrations, 44-45
marker paper, 33
markers, 32
markets, 4, 16
Marty, André, 30
masking tape, use of to draw patterns, 43
mass market, 4, 16
    adapting styles for the, 22, 23
materials, illustration, 32-33
McCardell, Claire, 21
media
    alternative, for collage, 48
    mixed, 52-53
men's wear, 16, 40

Michelangelo, 36
Milan, 20
mini-skirts, 8
Missoni, 27
Miyake, Issey, 21, 27
model, fashion see fashion model
money management 57
Montana, Claude, 27
mood, of a drawing, 31
Mori, Hanae, 27
mounting, of illustrations, 54-55
Mugler, Thierry, 20, 27
Muir, Jean, 27

New Look, The, 7, 8
New Romantic look, 9
newspapers, working for, 56
New York, 21

oil pastels, 33
Oldfield, Bruce, 21, 28
outline
    in collage, 48
    in mixed media, 52
overworking, 41, 53
Oxford bags, 6

packaging, working for, 56
paint brushes, 34
paper
    sizes, 35
    stretching, 35
    types of, 33
Paris, 20
pastel illustration, 42-43, 50-51
Pastel paper, 33
pastels
    artist's, 32
    oil, 33
Patou, Jean, 28
pattern, 10
    making, 12, 13
pattern cutter, 13
    career information, 58
patterns, how to draw, 43
pedal pushers, 8

pencil illustration, 50-51
pencils, 33
    coloured, 32
    Chinagraph, 33
photographer, fashion see fashion
    photographer
portfolio, 55, 57
pose, of figure in illustration, 31, 40
position, of figure in illustration, 40
poster paint, 32
presentation, of illustrations, 54-55
proportion, in figure drawing, 39
public relations consultant, career
    information, 59
punk fashion, 9
putty rubber, 34

Quant, Mary, 8, 28

rah-rah skirt, 9, 23
ready-to-wear, 4
    collections, 19, 20
Rhodes, Zandra, 21, 28

Saint Laurent, Yves, 20, 28
sample dress, 13
sample machinist, 12
Schiaparelli, Elsa, 28
scrap book, making a, 31
sculptures, using as models, 36
seasons, fashion, 10, 11, 18, 19
self-portraits, 36
shading, 50
sidelines, 57
sketching
    designs, 12
    illustrations, 45
skin tones, how to paint, 47
smudgers, 34
smudging, 34, 51
specializing, 16-17
spirit, petrol-based, 34
sports wear, 16, 40
spying, on collections, 22
street style, 21
stretching paper, 35

studio
    expanding, 17
    working in a, 10-11, 12-13
style, developing a, 41
stylist, career information, 59
sugar paper, 33

Tarlazzi, Angelo, 28
teacher, career information, 58
Teddy boys, 8
teenage fashion, 8, 16
template, 48
textile designer, career information, 58
texture, how to draw, 33, 44, 47, 53
theme, choosing a, 11, 18
tissue paper, 33, 48
toile, 12, 13
Tokyo, 21
tone, in illustration, 44, 51, 53
transparent covers, 55
trends, 11, 22, 56

Ungaro, Emanuel, 29
unisex fashion, 8, 9

Valentino, 20, 29
Versace, Gianni, 20, 29
video, using ideas from, 31
Vionnet, Madeleine, 7, 21

watercolour illustration, 42-43
watercolour paint, 32
watercolour paper, 33
water-soluble crayons, 32
water-soluble pencils, 32
wax crayons, 32, 43
Westwood, Vivienne, 9, 21, 29
window mounting, 54
women's wear, 16, 40
Worth, House of, 29

Yamamoto, Yohji, 9, 29
year, fashion see fashion year
Yuki, 29

Zoran, Ladicorbic, 29

Acknowledgements

We would like to thank all of the designers, companies and individuals who so generously allowed us to reproduce the illustrations and photographs listed as follows:

cover photographs, top left: Yves Saint Laurent (photographer Niall McInerney), top right: Emanuel Ungaro (photographer Niall McInerney); page 3, centre left: Betty Jackson (photographer Niall McInerney), bottom left: courtesy of Mr Marc Massin; page 4, courtesy of British Courtelle Awards; page 6, bottom left: courtesy of Chanel, bottom right: courtesy of Illustrated London News Picture Library; page 7, courtesy of Dior; page 8, courtesy of Mary Quant; page 9, Rei Kawakubo for Comme des Garçons (photographer Peter Lindbergh); page 17, courtesy of London College of Fashion (photographer David Whittington-Jones); page 20, Milan: Gianfranco Ferre (photographer Niall McInerney), Paris: Karl Lagerfeld (photographer Niall McInerney); page 21, London: courtesy of Katharine Hamnett, New York: Donna Karan (photographer Pierre Sherman), Tokyo: Issey Miyake (photographer Niall McInerney); page 24, top: Giorgio Armani (photographer Aldo Fallai), centre: Pierre Balmain, courtesy of Pierre Balmain et Cie, bottom: courtesy of Chanel; page 25, top: design drawing by Marc Bohan for Dior, centre: courtesy of Gianfranco Ferre, bottom: Bill Gibb (photographer John Adriaan); page 26, top: Betty Jackson (photographer Niall McInerney), centre left: Norma Kamali (photographer Niall McInerney), centre right: Donna Karan (photographer Pierre Sherman), bottom: Rei Kawakubo for Comme des Garçons (photographer Steven Meisle); page 27, top: Ralph Lauren (photographer Bruce Weber), centre: Claude Montana (photographer Niall McInerney), bottom: Jean Muir (photographer Michael Barrett); page 28, top left: Dinny Hall for Bruce Oldfield (photographer John Carter), top right: courtesy of House of Patou, centre left: courtesy of Mary Quant*, centre right: Jill Green for Zandra Rhodes (photographer Robyn Beeche), bottom: Yves Saint Laurent (photographer Niall McInerney); page 29, top: Gianni Versace (photographer Niall McInerney), centre left and right: courtesy of Mr Marc Massin, bottom: Yohji Yamamoto (photographer Niall McInerney); page 30, left: copyright Sevenarts Ltd, courtesy of Harper's Bazaar (British edition), right: courtesy of Mr Marc Massin.

* Whilst every effort was made to trace the photographer of these designs, his/her identity was still unknown at the time of going to press.